The Power of One

The Power of One

Theological Reflections on Loneliness

ANETTE EJSING

CASCADE *Books* · Eugene, Oregon

THE POWER OF ONE
Theological Reflections on Loneliness

Cascade Books
An Imprint of Wipf and Stock Publishers
199 W. 8th Ave., Suite 3
Eugene, OR 97401

www.wipfandstock.com

ISBN 13: 978-1-60608-549-3

Cataloging-in-Publication data:

Ejsing, Anette.

The power of one : theological reflections on loneliness / Anette Ejsing.

xiv + 104 p. ; 23 cm. — Includes bibliographical references.

ISBN 13: 978-1-60608-549-3

1. Loneliness — Religious aspects — Christianity. 2. Spiritual life — Christianity. I. Title.

BV4911 .E37 2011

Manufactured in the U.S.A.

To my friends

"It is sown in weakness, it is raised in power."

1 Corinthians 15:43

Contents

Preface

I WAS ORIGINALLY WORKING on two separate book manuscripts—one about solitude and one about the problem of evil. I was thinking that solitude is a good thing because it gives us rest and equips us to live meaningful lives with others. Evil is not a good thing, I was thinking, because it destroys life.

Somehow I wanted the book on solitude to answer the problem of evil. I wanted to know that when I rest in God's presence, it repairs all the damage evil has done to me. Experience of evil is something we will never understand and cannot avoid, but to find peace in God's presence helps us walk through them without giving evil the last word. This is what I was thinking.

Then I started questioning my own thinking. I asked myself, "Are solitude and evil really each other's opposites? Is one really designed to heal the other?"

The question became important because I realized no matter how fulfilling our experiences of solitude are, they always make us lonely if they do not come to an end. I have always been dissatisfied with variations of the argument "I am alone, but not lonely." Many writers on religion and spirituality argue that being alone may look unattractive, but in reality it is not. They say we just need to learn how we can turn loneliness into solitude.

I wanted to agree with them, and I wanted their argument to be true. It is just that I could not agree, because I had never met a person who did not become lonely if he or she spent too much time alone. There was no way around it. My own conclusion was that if solitude does not stop, and if we have to be alone for too long, we become lonely.

I know, of course, that we need the ability to rest and to be at peace with ourselves. Time in solitude and being alone in the presence of God teaches us this. If we do not have this ability, then we must develop it. Otherwise we will drive people crazy with all kinds of unhealthy attachment needs. Even Jesus lived by this principle and gave very high priority to regularly withdrawing from other people so he could be in the presence of God the Father.

Yet, I was beginning to think we lack evidence that Jesus' times of solitude were perfect alternatives to a life where evil destroys good things and daily demands draw us away from God. We tend to think that life would not be so difficult if only we could connect with God the way Jesus did. Then we would be more in tune with God, we tell ourselves. But, why are we so sure this is what Jesus experienced in God's presence? Perhaps his time in solitude with God involved deep sorrow because it reinforced his experience of *separation* from God. How do we know solitude did not make Jesus more intensely aware of his loneliness in this world?

Those were the thoughts that challenged me to redefine the relationship between solitude and the problem of evil. In the end I concluded that the problem of loneliness is a concrete example of the more general problem of evil. Like all other evil, loneliness is something we do not have the power to shake off. It is something we do not understand. In fact, if we consult loneliness researchers in the hope that they can help us understand the evil of loneliness, they tell us we do not know what loneliness is. Even more interesting to me is the discovery that loneliness follows us into God's presence and shapes the experience of solitude we have with him—just like all other forms of evil follow us everywhere we go. I mean, can you honestly say you never feel lonely when you are alone with God?

This all-pervasive sense of loneliness makes me think that we would enjoy fellowship with God so much more if people we love were part of the experience. Not just the way we can be part of each other's lives when we "share our day" with one another. Rather, if we had access to unbroken social interaction with others, then we would all be part of each other's experience of God. We would be *together* in God's presence, not alone in God's presence. There would be no distance between us and we would have no need to talk about the experience of God, because it would be an essential part of our relationship with each other. Other people would be a natural part of our experience with God and we would be a natural part of theirs. In that situation, nothing would be more enjoyable than being together in God's presence.

Think about it. All biblical images of heaven are communal (banquet, city, wedding). They are not about being alone with God and enjoying time away from other people. When I contemplate these communal images, it occurs to me that the only place I will be alone with God after this life is when he asks me to tell the story of my life. He will then ask me whether or not I desire to live in community with his people and himself. If this is what I want, it is what I will get and, past that point, I will never be alone again.

The way our world works, however, makes it impossible for us to have such intimate fellowship with each other. If we are honest, I am sure many of us would say that we prefer some distance to most other people. This is exactly my point, because our world makes it impossible to have a permanently satisfying experience of fellowship, both with other people and with God. Being alone is a necessary part of life as we know it.

For now, therefore, what we can do is to withdraw from others, spend time in God's presence, and learn from him what it means to find pleasure in simple and quiet fellowship. We call it solitude, and it is the best we can do under our circumstances of life. We only need to remember that it will never be a perfect alternative to a life infected with the experience of loneliness—just as Jesus often withdrew from other people to be with the Father, but still had to live with loneliness as a fundamental life circumstance. How else can we make sense of the reality that he was fully human and had to live in separation from God?

With these reflections in mind, I started thinking about the power of loneliness. I wondered if loneliness might not be one of the driving forces of Jesus' life. Could it be that the power by which he changed the world hinged on his willingness to embrace his loneliness? Could it be that solitude is where he learned to face and accept the loneliness of existence in this world? The most powerful moment of his life was, after all, when he was dying and did not understand why God was absent. Maybe he was able to accept God's absence on the cross only because he had already accepted his loneliness in solitude with God?

If this is the case, then consider our belief that it was in his death that Jesus broke the power of evil. Then all of a sudden it looks like there is an intimate connection between solitude and the reality of evil—much more intimate than we perhaps tend to think. Solitude may still be the answer to the problem of evil, and it may still repair all the damage evil has done to us—but not because it is a perfect alternative or a place where the powers of evil cannot reach us. Rather, it is the answer because solitude is where we draw into God's presence and learn to embrace the suffering of loneliness that we all have to deal with because we are separated from God by the power of evil.

In the end, then, I wrote *The Power of One* because I want us to stop telling each other that loneliness is not so bad. It is bad. But I also wrote this book because I want us to start telling each other that if we decide to walk through this valley of loneliness, then we also have the opportunity to trust that God will release his redemptive power through us—just as he did through Jesus when he died and did not understand why God was absent. God is in the business of bringing new life through the experience of death. So, if loneliness is a kind of death, why not learn how to tap into it as a source of new life?

Acknowledgments

Thanks to everyone who gave critical and constructive feedback on different versions of the manuscript for this book. I have loved every minute of engagement with you, either in person, over the phone, in writing, via online social media, through interaction as colleagues, in classrooms and church settings, or at professional conferences and meetings where you challenged me to revise my thinking about theology, loneliness, and what to do about it all. I sincerely hope our conversation about this topic will not stop here, but rather continue to grow into the future.

To editors and staff at Wipf and Stock Publishers, thank you for insight, support, and patience. You exude energy.

My deepest thanks is reserved for my friends, whom I would never trade for anything in this world. You are my conversation partners and the most important reason I have tasted the true meaning of human fellowship. You engage me, challenge me, and never give up on me. Plus, you make yourselves available in a way that pushes our dialogue forward over time. I am not sure how you do it, but when we talk about old things, it never turns into a rehearsal of the same old points. Something new always emerges. This has been true in our conversations about loneliness, too, and for that I am particularly thankful. Loneliness is hard pressed in your company.

INTRODUCTION

ONE IS A POWERFUL number. If you ask mathematicians, they tell you the universe is built on the principle of one because it is the most basic unit we have. You can only have two, five thousand, or several trillion of anything if you are able to add up enough individual ones. This becomes more interesting when you realize we cannot prove that one really is one. We assume it is true, and going on this assumption works well. Even though all scientific progress is based on this mathematical assumption, however, we have no proof that one is one. This says something about the power of one.

Christianity is based on the power of one, too. There is "one Lord, one faith, one baptism."[1] God is one. Jesus is the only (one) Son of God. God first created one man and one woman. Plus, God does not care for people like you. He cares for you, the one that is you and who is no one else.

Many dislike this about Christianity because it makes it an exclusive religion. They ask how you can claim that the Judeo-Christian God is the only true God. Why did God choose one people, the Hebrews, and why did he give them status over other people? Why is Jesus elevated over all other great religious leaders in history? Why is Peter singled out among the disciples to hold the key to the kingdom? And why does Jesus talk so favorably about the one lost sheep as opposed to the ninety nine that are not lost?

I did not acknowledge the significance of these questions until it became clear that America was sliding into serious economic recession in 2008. Everybody watched in near-panic how the job loss numbers escalated more rapidly than they had at any other point in our generation. What did this mean for praying believers? If there are sixty jobs and seventy unemployed individuals, an omnipotent God must acknowledge the discrepancy of ten jobs. Even God is subject to the logic of the universe he created. If I need a job, then, and know God loves my unemployed neighbor as much as he loves me, is it not selfish to pray that God will give me the job ahead of someone else?

Maybe this question haunted me the way guilt always haunts us in the privileged West, when we are reminded of the underprivileged among us. Even so, there is something about mathematical logic that complicates the idea of prayer when you apply it to things like unemployment numbers. In other words, it is a challenge to a praying believer that two plus two always equals four.

It had never been difficult for me to ask God for things in the past when I knew receiving them would not happen at someone else's expense. As a graduate student, God would provide what I needed, almost effortlessly and sometimes miraculously. I would like to connect professionally with a scholar in my field but was afraid to pursue it, and one day I coincidentally ran into him. I did not have a place to live, and an elderly couple I meet in the grocery story invited me to come live with them for free. I needed $300 for an expense I could not cover, and someone unexpectedly handed me a check for $300. I could not afford a flight ticket to go overseas for two family events I desired to attend. They were within two months of each other, and I received an invitation to give a talk in my family's area during the week of each event, airfare covered.

These are all real situations where God met my need in response to prayer. Still, in the world where I lived, there was generally enough to go around, and I never thought about guilt or being favored over others because God honored my petition. Not until the recession.

THE POWER OF ONE

I came across this statement at some point after the recession had become a reality: "Welfare is for a purpose . . . whereas Christian love is for a person."[2] This is something Mother Teresa apparently enjoyed saying to people who wondered about her work with the poor in Calcutta's slum. She always focused on the individual and ascribed no special significance to things like politics and social-welfare systems. She never helped the poor as such, always only the poor individual person.

Many saw this, and some described her attitude as narrow-minded and medically irresponsible. In a sharp voice, Christopher Hitchens criticizes her ministry as deliberately promoting "neglect of what is commonly understood as proper medicine or care."[3] It is true that she would sometimes take on a medical case that needed more expertise than she possessed, and this could result in misdiagnosis and inappropriate medication. Meanwhile, she kept insisting that her job was to "sell love," to one person at a time, not to be a medical professional. This is a serious critique and should not be uncritically dismissed.

At the same time, there is something powerful about Mother Teresa's ability to focus on that one objective which was to extend God's love to individual persons. Reality is that if she had not pursued that objective, then "her poor" would have died an even poorer death. Add to this that she used Holy Communion as her most important source of personal nourishment. She had a constant yearning for Christ's body and blood, to the extent that, on her death-bed, a Hindu doctor requested the actual presence of the Eucharist in her room because it calmed her physically. When you hold these things together, there is something like a "pattern of one" to her lifestyle. She was "the one" for the poor, she brought "the one" into her care, and she fed on "the one" for herself.

Another illustration of the power of one is the Christian claim that God became incarnate. Consider the fact that all Christological controversies, then and now, converge in the outrageous act of communication of idioms (*communicatio idiomatum*). When we say about this one person, Jesus Christ, "he is fully and truly human" and also say, "he is fully and truly divine," our words do not make sense. We are predicating one and the same person with two different natures. Within the parameters of all logic, this is not possible. Either the person of Christ was human or he was divine. Or he was human some of the time, and divine the rest of the time. That one thing can always only be one thing at one time is as necessary now as it was then. It can never be two things at the same time.

Of course, we can accept by faith that Christ had a double nature and was both human and divine all the time. If we do this, however, we only demonstrate one more time how difficult it is to override the power of one. It requires faith. Believing in something like Christ being both human and divine is a choice of faith. But, as we already know, so is believing in the mathematical axiom that "one is one." Therefore, whether we talk about Christ or about mathematical axioms, it will always involve an act of faith.

Personally, I experience the power of one when I discover that God loves me as a person, not as a purpose. Again, remember the recession and the high unemployment numbers that followed in its wake. When I first looked at my unemployed friends, I wondered about the logic of available workers against available jobs. Then I thought about Jesus' comment to one of his disciples who had the same kind of concern for one of his friends. Jesus said to this disciple, "If I want him to remain alive . . . what is that to you?"[4] Maybe I needed to learn from this that I must trust God for myself without comparing my needs to the needs of others. I can care for my friends, and they can care for me, but neither of us has access to that place within each other where we trust God for ourselves. If we want to experience God's provision, then our only option is to accept that God relates to individual persons in ways that dispense with logic.

This lack of logic in the divine economy sheds light on another aspect of the power of one. I am thinking of the impact we can have on the world when we discover the value God places on the individual person. Think about those who have changed the course of history because they had the courage to stand out. Of course, no individual person can become a reformer without the support of devoted followers. But, no resistance movement can get off the ground without a strong and courageous individual at the keel. That person must have the courage to take much the same position Martin Luther did when he stood up at the Diet of Worms and, against the corruption in the Catholic Church, supposedly ended his speech with these words: "Here I stand. I can do no other. God help me."

Rosa Parks, the civil rights activist, is another more contemporary example of an individual who changed history because she had the courage to stand out. She knew she was exactly as valuable as any other person, and therefore sat down in a bus seat for which others considered her unworthy. And then she just kept sitting there. The anti-apartheid activist Nelson Mandela is a third example. The price he ended up paying for his views on racial equality was twenty-seven years in prison. This is a lot, but he was willing because he was courageous enough to stand out. We could also mention the French national heroine, Joan of Arc, who had such confidence as a warrior that she took military charge and led the French army to victory against the English. Talk about standing up for one's beliefs.

Unfortunately, it is no easy process to acquire the kind of strength and influence these individuals had. Nor is it one you can decide to pursue in the manner you pursue other goals, like an education or a job, for instance. Plus, if we study their lives closely, we realize that they were no foreigners to experiences of loneliness. I even venture to say that loneliness is often a driving force behind the success of reformers. Except, at some point in the process of maturation, they learn to use loneliness as a resource of personal empowerment.

Along these lines, it is common knowledge that talented artists and thinkers often have painful life stories to tell. I am not sure why it is not as common to think of these individuals as lonely, but maybe it requires admitting that our accomplishments rarely reflect who we are at a deeper level. Henri Nouwen was not afraid to admit this and often talked about the fact that pain has an isolating effect on us. Condensing his thoughts into a question, he asked: "Does not all creativity ask for a certain encounter with our loneliness?"[5] This is true for people of great talent, but I think it is true for all of us at some level. If we are courageous enough to admit it, and bold enough to talk about it, I am sure we will discover just how common it is to struggle with loneliness.

Let us therefore be careful not to make premature conclusions when we admire historical figures and wish to be like them. They inspire us, but we need to keep in mind that, more often than not, they know what it means to struggle with loneliness. So, if we desire to make a difference in our world, it looks like we could use this insight constructively and admit that we need to get in touch with our own loneliness. The most unattractive aspect of this strategy is, of course, that it will hurt.

We do not like to be lonely, we hate to admit it, and we are ashamed of it when we do. Instead, we try everything we can to avoid loneliness. We even exchange loneliness for other unpleasant things, such as bad company, addictive habits, or dysfunctional relationships. The irony is that a dysfunctional relationship, for instance, hurts as much as it does to face one's own loneliness. It might be a different kind of hurting, but it hurts nonetheless. So, why not choose the pain of loneliness over the pain of an escape solution, like a dysfunctional relationship? If we can turn loneliness into an opportunity to make a difference in our world, then we owe it to ourselves to think about possible ways of doing this.

A good place to start is to acknowledge that facing our loneliness will make us feel worse before it makes us feel better. Let me return to Rosa Parks to illustrate what I mean. As a black person in a society of segregation and white supremacy, she must have been familiar with loneliness. She must have known what it is like to be as unwanted as the food you push aside on your plate because you do not like it. Segregation must have pushed her aside that way, and it must have created a sense of loneliness in her. But, she was immensely courageous when she made the intentional choice to sit down in that bus seat and was arrested for it. It made her loneliness visible to others and must have intensified her sense of loneliness. At first. Because her act of intentional resistance against loneliness, by an act of loneliness, made a different impact over time. It turned the world she loved into a less lonely place for the people she loved.

I am convinced Rosa Parks had the courage to do what she did because she believed so strongly in a world of racial equality that she felt something like this: "Here I sit. I can do no other. God help me." She must have fixed her eyes intently on the truth of racial equality, even though it was not real in the world where she lived. With hope, she must have believed that her segregation was not God's truth about her, and that it could not possibly be God's desire for her. The power of that belief was released because she focused so strongly on it that history had no other choice but to yield to the pressure of her action. It had to stop devaluing people based on the tone of their skin color and it had to start bending according to her belief.

This is a very Christian way to live one's life. Indeed, St. Paul tells us that not only racial equality but salvation and eternal life depend on willingness to risk oneself for the sake of hope: "For by hope we are saved ... if we hope for what we do not see, we wait for it with patience."[6] If we dig a little deeper into the theology behind this idea, however, we find that Christian hope is quite different from optimism—because it depends on willingness to suffer.

In my experience, this willingness usually comes to a test when life circumstances impose suffering upon us. We may, for instance, want to pursue a military career because we like the idea of making sacrifices for our country, perhaps even the sacrifice of our own life. But then we develop a disease that incapacitates us physically and the military is no longer an option. Gone is the luxury of choosing the sacrifice we would like to make, and then we face a much more difficult choice. We must decide whether or not we will relinquish control and put our hope in an invisible God whose provisions we do not understand. Yes, we have everything through Christ, but what if God does not act as we believe he will?

This is where the rubber meets the road for believers. Especially when loneliness is part of the life circumstances that are beyond our power to change. Then we must respond to our loneliness with the attitude Christ had when he faced death and God was nowhere to be found. Hence, it seems like we may just as well acknowledge the reality of our own loneliness before circumstances force us, so there is no way around the process of telling our loneliness stories. You must tell yours and I must tell mine.

TELLING YOUR STORY

Maybe you remember struggling with loneliness when you moved away from home and started college. You had longed to leave home because your family was becoming old news. Even so, the new world of college came at you with such overwhelming force that it could not become a new home for you. Or maybe you are now married but experience a growing distance between yourself and the person you had hoped would be your soul mate and ally for life. Or financial difficulties have caused conflicts in your family and you feel estranged from the people who used to be your supporters. Maybe you are unemployed and feel lost in a society that no longer needs you. Or you have a successful career and your colleagues are your closest friends, but you know they would leave you for a better job elsewhere. Perhaps serious illness, or a death in the family, isolates you from others. Or you have experienced divorce, are going through one right now, or have divorced parents, and this makes it hard for you to be close to others, even though that is what you desire most.

All these scenarios involve experiences of loneliness. They may be temporary or they may be more permanent. Whatever the situation, your loneliness story belongs to the greater story of your life, and you must include it if someone asks you to give an honest account of your life.

If loneliness has been an unusually large part of your life, you may even say that loneliness *is* the story of your life. If this is the case, here is my response: you do not know what you are talking about. Not because you do not know what happened to you in the past, but because you do not know what will happen to you in the future. As long as you keep breathing, your story remains unfinished. You anticipate certain things about the days to come, but you do not know how much of it will actually happen. Because you are in no position to tell your life story in full.

Or maybe you are? Consider the fact that your story covers a relatively short period of time that fits into the much longer story of all history. There was the pre-historic era, antiquity, the Middle Ages, Renaissance, and Modernity. Think of these historical eras as pieces that make up God's story. Imagine that one part of this story, Modernity, takes up one chapter, somewhere toward the late middle of God's story. Then listen to what

Scott Bader-Saye says about the majority of people whose stories are told prior to this chapter:

> [They] believed the world had a story because the world had an author. History is God's story, they would have said, and while humans are capable of creating confusion during the middle scenes of the drama, God never ceases to guide and direct the creation to its good end. The plotline may seem vague at times, even threatened, but it never devolves into chaos or randomness.[7]

Something interesting happens when you start looking at your personal story as a part of God's story. It allows you to tell your own story in full, while it is still unfinished. This sounds like a paradox, and it is. But when you look at your present life in light of the end God already has in mind for all history, then you know there is also a goal for you to reach. Then you get the sense that your story is moving in the direction of God's end.

In practical terms, it makes you less fearful and less lonely because it gives you confidence about the things that will happen in the future. You no longer give as much attention to yourself and your current situation because your eyes are fixed on the future. Plus, it liberates you from that frustrating tendency we all have to start backsliding. When we stop focusing on the future, it happens almost immediately that we begin to slide backward into the past. From experience, we all know that it is nearly impossible to be happy in the present moment unless we hope for something good in the future.

Dietrich Bonhoeffer had a good eye for this when he ended his second dissertation on the note that "they ... who desire to be defined by the present, fall subject to the past, to themselves, death and guilt."[8] He said this because he believed that motion is an essential element of human life. If sliding backward involves losing joy in the present moment, then Bonhoeffer was right to also comment that, "It is only out of the future that the present can be lived."[9] One can only imagine how often he had to live on his own hope for a better future in order to survive the loneliness of his imprisonment under the Nazi regime in Germany.

In case you are intrigued and want to experiment with telling your personal loneliness story with God's future in mind, there are some things you need to believe in order to succeed. First, you must embrace the premodern belief that all of history is God's story. Second, you must believe that God has a good end in mind as he is writing this story. Third, you must believe that the end of your personal story and the end of historical time are somehow related and that both take place beyond historical time as we know it. If you do not believe these things, I invite you to pretend that you do. After you finish reading this book, you can decide whether or not you want to keep believing it. You have time.

TELLING MY STORY

I should not ask you to tell your story in light of God's future for you, unless I am ready to tell my own. By nature loneliness is a personal matter, and no theological reflections on loneliness can be persuasive if they do not include a story about the personal experience of it.

In my case, two kinds of loneliness have been more challenging than others, and my story keeps unfolding as I struggle with these. Over time, this struggle has introduced me to a third kind of loneliness in my life and all three are such strong forces in my life that I have chosen to structure this book around them. In fact, writing this book quickly turned into an opportunity for me where I could gain a better understanding of my own loneliness.

I now agree with Nouwen who went through very deep personal struggles and said this about them: "by following them to their roots, I was touching a level where they could be shared."[10] I see my own writing process reflected in this comment. It started out with a narrow focus on my own loneliness, but eventually found its way to the roots where I believe the problem of loneliness disappears into the fertile soil of Christian theology. The result is a book on the power it releases in us when we have the courage to embrace the most perplexing experiences of loneliness, namely romantic, spiritual, and social loneliness.

The first kind of loneliness I know personally relates to the fact that I have never been married and have never lived in a committed long-term relationship. Regardless of my attempts to approach the single lifestyle with a positive attitude, living without a life partner always involved a certain kind of loneliness.

The second kind of loneliness relates to my twelve years as a foreigner in America. When your legal status is that of being a residential guest in a foreign country, it involves a certain kind of loneliness. You do not walk on the soil of your geographical homeland and are not surrounded by your own people. This makes you lonely. When things like your first language, the landscape of your youth, your humor, culture, moral sensibility, and political discourse do not match those around you, a fundamental sense of social disconnect eventually creeps up on you. In my case, being a foreigner was always reinforced by the fact that I was the only person in my family living in America.

Make no mistake of it. These two identities—single and foreigner—are also the primary drives behind an adventurous lifestyle I would never trade, and here is why. I have no family to hold me back from going places, doing things, and pursuing opportunities I find attractive. I can do what I want, when I want, and in the way I want. This means that I generally travel a lot, have no problem moving for a good job, can pursue interesting dating relationships, and now have wonderful friends in cool places. Interestingly, many of my married and geographically settled friends often express a secret desire to live this kind of life. They are attracted to the intensity of it, which is something they cannot have because commitments to family and property bind them financially.

Still, loneliness is easily my enemy number one. Which brings me to the third and most painful kind of loneliness I know from personal experience. It has to do with faith. Over the years, I have intentionally asked God for marriage and a sense of social, or geographical, belonging. God has not given me these two things, and at some point this started to give me a feeling of running up against a heavy and thick firewall that separated me spiritually from God. It never caused me to lose faith, but it did cause me to feel that God was withholding from me what I need in order to thrive at the most fundamental human level.

The more smoothly and even miraculously God has provided me with other things I have asked for, the harder it has been to understand why he has chosen to withhold marriage and social belonging. At first, it was frustrating and I did what all frustrated people do. I made stupid decisions in order to fix my problem, only to realize that they did not work. Slowly and reluctantly, I had to accept that my efforts were mostly in vain and did not facilitate much positive change. As this became clear to me, something else was happening, too. I experienced a painful and growing sense of permanency to my loneliness. It started to solidify and, as I became aware of this, I fell to a new level of loneliness. Or maybe it is more accurate to say that I experienced a kind of loneliness I had never experienced before. It was the loneliness of looking for God in all the places I knew, but without finding him.

It was at this point that I became more intentionally curious about loneliness as something other than just my personal problem. I did not understand the problem of loneliness but wanted to, so I began asking other people about theirs. This quickly opened my eyes to the reality that most of us are extremely uncomfortable talking about personal loneliness. It was almost humorous to watch some of my friends draw a sigh of relief when I changed the topic and asked about their financial situation, sex life, or political views. I concluded that we need to approach loneliness as a taboo.

In any case, I now see that I started writing this book because I needed to tell my own loneliness story. It began as a story of lament and a confused need for the healing of my loneliness, but it took on a life of its own. It turned into a story where I discovered that if we bring our loneliness out of denial and into the light, it eventually reveals a powerful underside. For me, this revelation could not happen until I accepted that my loneliness story does not have the final word in my life.

Obviously, this only goes to show that I did not know what I was talking about when I first complained that loneliness was the story of my life. It also showed me that a personal story really can change when we tell it from the perspective of God's end for us. Mine did not change the way I had hoped it would, and God's view of my loneliness was not the one I wanted to find. But that is how it goes when we allow God's story to enter our own. We know the end of that story from the beginning, but somehow it reveals itself more fully when we start following God into our own future. What a mystery that we can know the end of a journey and then, when we get there, it looks like an entirely different end, although it is still the same.

Before I introduce the three main chapters of this book, we should remind ourselves that we need help in order to tell our story accurately. Not because we intend to get our stories wrong when we tell them, but because it is difficult for us to get them right.

Help! We Cannot Tell Our Stories

We deceive ourselves all the time. We need to, because otherwise all the complexities of life would be too overwhelming. As a matter of giving order and coherence to it all, we therefore fix up the story of our life. Telling and believing that story helps explain and connect all the different experiences we have. It helps us find meaning in life and it helps us stay healthy.

You know it from your professional life. Your supervisor makes a decision you do not understand and maybe do not agree with. You wonder what is happening, but when you create a story around it, and plot your experience into that story, things begin to make sense. It may go something like this: "My supervisor does not recognize my gifts and my skills. My resources remain untapped and I am not working to my full potential. But I can see why, because she is not the right person for the job. She does not have what it takes to draw out the best in me." This is your story and it may be right. Or it may be wrong. Most likely, it is a little of both, but it gives meaning to your experience and you regain a sense of control over the situation. You know where you stand in relation to your supervisor, because you believe your story. And then you can move on.

Even though plotting our experiences into a story helps us stay healthy, we cannot deceive ourselves too much, because then we lose touch with reality. Not only that, but it keeps us from living authentic lives and it keeps us from knowing what we are doing with our lives. Stanley Hauerwas makes this point when he says that "our ability to know what we are up to and live authentically depends on our capacity to avoid self-deception."[11] So, he advises us to adjust our stories so they reflect reality accurately. This is very difficult because it means letting go of false beliefs. It is so difficult, in fact, that only a few of us are willing to do it. We would not really believe something if we could just as well *not* believe it, would we?

Now, let us say we are courageous enough to change our story so it accurately reflects reality. Then we face another challenge, which is that we self-deceive again. In spite of our good intentions, every time we correct our story, the new story will be infected by self-deception too. Apparently, we need help to tell our story. Hauerwas suggests looking for that help in the story of the gospel. It is a story that tells us we cannot be righteous on our own, and righteous is exactly what we are trying to be when we keep adjusting our story. The gospel will help us admit that our retelling is mostly about adding new layers of self-deception to old ones. Hauerwas' most astute point is that we might as well accept the gospel voluntarily before the web of our self-deceptive stories complicates our lives so much that they begin to disintegrate.[12]

Now, telling God's story about us means stepping out of the comfort zone of what we can see. It means throwing ourselves into a situation where we relinquish control and wait for God to fulfill his promises. No believer can possibly know what this waiting experience will be like. It may be short and intense, or long and persistent. It may be full of joy and anticipation, or it may test the limits of our hope. Your waiting experience may not feel like much of a challenge, or it may be more than you feel you can handle. In the midst of all this, one thing is certain: you will find yourself suspended between trust and doubt, and all you can do is wait.

Waiting for God to fulfill his promises is the heartbeat of Christian faith and very different from the cognitive cycle of self-deception we need to break. It is another way to point us, the lonely ones, in the direction of the power of one, because it strengthens in us the capacity to trust that God will release his redemptive power through us.

THE POWER OF THREE: A WORD ABOUT
THE STRUCTURE OF THIS BOOK

The Christian God is both one and three. If we want to focus on the power of one, we should therefore also focus on the power of three. This quickly gets complicated, however, because it can launch us into exhausting discussions of the philosophical technicalities behind the idea "three in one." I suggest we assume the early theologians were right when they concluded that God is, as they formulated it, "one being in three persons." Then I suggest looking at the theological significance of the number three, which explains why I structure *The Power of One* by three main chapters.

Not only theologians think there is power in the number three. I became aware of this after I saw a documentary film about Bob Dylan, and he claimed that counting to three is musically more powerful than counting to four. He did not explain why, so I dipped into the literature on pattern numbers. I was surprised to realize the many ways we communicate in the pattern of three. In the Greek, Roman, Modern European, and American cultures, the numerical category of three is quite significant. Consider the following sets of three, for example. Hip, Hip, Hooray. A minister, a priest, and a rabbi. Quarterback, halfback, and fullback. Wine, women, and song. Knife, fork, and spoon. Tall, dark, and handsome. Red, yellow, and green. Army, Navy, and Air Force. Past, present, and future. ABC. Blood, sweat, and tears.[13]

For Christian theologians, the preeminent example of the pattern of three is Father, Son, and Holy Spirit. Some are uncomfortable with this triad of three persons. They say it supports a patriarchal worldview and relies too heavily on a masculine image of God. Or they say it is oppressive to those who cannot identify with faith in a God who is limited to three expressions. Their discomfort does not automatically lead to a rejection of the theological significance of the pattern of three, however. Many of them argue that, rather than identifying God as Father, Son, and Holy Spirit, we should talk about God as creator, redeemer, and sustainer. Notice that this shifts the focus from God's personal being to the way God acts in the world. It affirms that God created the universe, became incarnate, and continues to sustain us, but it avoids talking about God's identity. I see some problems with this approach, but that is besides the point I wish to make here.

When I first started reflecting on loneliness in the context of faith, I had a vague sense that three kinds of loneliness were particularly challenging for Christian believers. I already briefly told the story of my personal experience with each of these: romantic, social, and spiritual loneliness. A few years later, I now have not only personal but also theological reasons to reflect on the significance of these three. More specifically, I reflect on them in light of the Christian confession that God created the world, redeemed it through Christ, and is now sustaining it by the Holy Spirit. Here follows an introduction of the way I connect these three acts with our experience of romantic, social, and spiritual loneliness.

Whether God acts as creator, redeemer, or sustainer, it always involves full participation of all three persons of God. Both Christ and the Holy Spirit were involved in the creation of the world, for instance. And both Christ and the Father are involved in the Spirit's work of sustaining the world. This is to say that we can easily distinguish the three different acts of God, but we cannot isolate them from each other without doing damage to the unity of God's three persons. We can never say we experience only one of the three persons acting in our lives. It is always all three acting in unison.[14]

Likewise, when we study different kinds of loneliness experience, it is easy to distinguish them but hard to isolate them from each other. How can we say, for instance, that we are definitely spiritually lonely but not socially lonely? Or that we are often socially lonely but never romantically lonely? As I illustrated in my own brief story, the experience I had of spiritual loneliness emerged out of experiences with romantic and social loneliness, and I cannot possibly say they are isolated phenomena in my life. They are clearly distinct, but they are all somehow part of the one experience that causes me to say, "I am lonely."

Robert S. Weiss helped me understand this complex identity of loneliness. Two decades ago, he noticed what still seems to hold true, namely that loneliness researchers are unable to give a precise definition of loneliness. Yes, he says, we can describe what loneliness feels like. We can explain "how the perception of emotional isolation is followed by a dull ache in one's chest, a sense of wanting to cry or of having cried, a need to search, and a high level of physiological mobilization."[15] But, when we try to define this experience, we know no better than to start talking about the things that caused it. It is easy for us to point to the reasons for our loneliness, but when it comes to defining our loneliness, we fall short. What is loneliness? We do not know. The only thing we can do is describe how it feels, and then we can give some reasons why we feel lonely.[16]

I am in no place to advance the field of loneliness research on this matter and admit to continuing the tradition of those who talk about the causes of loneliness rather than its definition. I also admit that I narrow my interest to theologically specific causes and leave it for experts in other fields to analyze causes that relate to their area of expertise. This is to say that I am interested in the promises I have through faith in the God who creates, redeems, and sustains, because these promises are directly tied to the things that have been causing loneliness in my life. In more specific terms, my faith in God implies three specific promises from God: exclusive fellowship with a partner, fellowship with Christ, and inclusive fellowship with other Christians. The fact that these three promises have remained unfulfilled is what has been driving my experiences of romantic, spiritual, and social loneliness.

Let me go into a little more detail about these causes. This will also introduce some important theological premises that support the argument of *The Power of One*. You may not subscribe to these premises, but in fairness to the case I want to make, you need to know what they are. Furthermore, this gives you the opportunity to critique my argument by critiquing the theology I espouse as I make it.

When God created the world, part of his act was to create human beings. He created two of them and in such a way that they were attracted to each other and found fulfillment by being together. To confess the belief that this is how God created human beings is to believe that God intends for us to find fulfillment in an exclusive relationship with another human being. If we do not have such a relationship, or if the one we have does not fulfill us, we experience what I call romantic loneliness. The more intense the experience, the more likely we are to question our belief and confession that God created us for the experience of fulfillment in an exclusive relationship. It is not the only way God created us for fulfillment, but it is an important one.

When God redeemed the world, it meant that human beings could now connect with God in a way it was impossible to do before that time. God became incarnate in Christ, died to save us from a life in bondage to sin, and rose again in order to give us eternal life. To confess the belief that this is how God brings us to himself is to believe that God desires fellowship with us and that he intends to be close to us, so we can be close to him. If we do not experience this kind of fellowship with God through Christ, we experience what I call spiritual loneliness. We feel lonely in relation to God and are likely to question our belief and confession that God desires fellowship with us.

When God decided to continue the effects of Christ's life, death, and resurrection by sending the Holy Spirit to live in us, it marked the beginning of God's third act. Through this act, God initiated the process of making his people one with each other and one with himself. Theologians refer to this sense of oneness as the fellowship of the Holy Spirit. To confess belief that the one spirit of God lives in all who love God, is to believe that all Christians are one with each other and united with God. If we somehow experience exclusion from the fellowship of all Christians, then we experience what I call social loneliness. We feel lonely in relation to other Christians and are likely to question our belief and confession that God unites us through our spiritual fellowship with all other believers.

If you hold the three previous paragraphs together, and keep in mind our struggle with romantic, spiritual, and social loneliness, then it adds up to this simple but challenging question: Why does the Christian faith not heal loneliness? If God promises us fellowship with a partner, with Christ, and with all his people, why are we still lonely in these areas? This is the driving question of *The Power of One*, and it leaves me at a point where I can now introduce the content of its three main chapters.

Chapter 1, "Romantic Loneliness and the Creation of Human Beings," first explains how I connect the experience of romantic loneliness with faith in God the creator. In this chapter, I focus on the story of Adam and Eve, which is the part of the Judeo-Christian creation story that concerns the origin of human beings. Doing this, I invite you to consider this question: Does marriage heal romantic loneliness? In the first part of chapter 1, I answer the question in the negative. To illustrate my answer, I tell the story of a couple who was married for thirty years but whose relationship did not heal the romantic loneliness that first drew them to each other. Theologically, I offer an interpretation of the story of Adam and Eve that supports my argument that marriage does not, cannot, and never was designed to heal romantic loneliness. In the second part of chapter 1, I develop the opposite argument and conclude that marriage in fact does heal romantic loneliness. I illustrate this argument through the examples of a married couple, a single man, and a celibate monk, all of whom experience and speak of spousal intimacy as something that makes them less lonely. Theologically, I support my argument by reference to John Paul II's interpretation of Adam's aloneness as he presents it in his *Theology of the Body*.

Chapter 2, "Spiritual Loneliness and Redemption in Christ," first describes God's incarnation in Christ as a direct, divine response to our spiritual loneliness. It then invites you to consider this question: Does Christ heal spiritual loneliness? In the first part of chapter 2, I tell the story of a friend who died a physically painful death. Even more painfully, his strong Christian faith was not enough to protect him against the experience that God was absent in his suffering as he died. This story illustrates my conclusion that Christ does not heal spiritual loneliness, despite the fact that he came to do exactly that. Theologically, I use Jürgen Moltmann's theology of the cross to support this conclusion. In the second part of chapter 2, I tell the story of Mother Teresa who suffered a lifelong sense of loneliness in relation to God. I use her story to illustrate my argument that Christ does in fact heal spiritual loneliness. Theologically, I support this argument by reference to the theology of suffering, especially Pope John Paul II's encyclical, *Salvifici Doloris*.

Chapter 3, "Social Loneliness and the Fellowship of the Holy Spirit," relies on social-scientific research to describe the American culture of loneliness. In this chapter, I suggest that the coming of the Holy Spirit is God's direct response to our social loneliness, and I tell my own story of life as a foreigner in America. I then ask this question: Does the Fellowship of the Holy Spirit heal social loneliness? In the first part of chapter 3,

I answer this question in the negative and illustrate it with a personal story of the social loneliness I observed in a vibrant church fellowship. Theologically, I rely on Dietrich Bonhoeffer's theology of sociality to argue that the fellowship of the Holy Spirit cannot possibly heal social loneliness. In the second part of chapter 3, I come to the opposite conclusion, that the fellowship of Christians does in fact heal social loneliness. To illustrate this second argument of chapter 3, I use the story of my own conversion experience. Theologically, I support this conclusion by reference to the passionate dispute between Karl Barth and Emil Brunner over the concept of what they called the *Anknüpfungspunkt*.

Finally, in the Conclusion, I return to my own experience with romantic, social and spiritual loneliness. I tell the story of how loneliness kept pushing me into despair, but how my joy was eventually restored. The end of the story is not that my loneliness went away, but that joy convinced me of the privilege of the lonely. It is therefore my final point that St. Paul speaks of this privilege when he encourages us to find joy in our sufferings. Finding this joy, I argue, is where we make contact with the power of one.

This brings me to the final point I need to make before I invite you to read the main chapters of this book. It concerns my use of the term *power* and what I mean by it.

We generally situate ourselves in the world by the power we have. We are below those who have more power than us, and we are above those who have less. Power is leverage and we use it to put ourselves and each other in place. That is, we use our power to position ourselves as individuals in a world full of other individuals. Our power fluctuates over time because we may not have as much power today as we had ten years ago. Or we may have more. Our power also fluctuates with the relationships we have. We may have significant power when we are with one group of people, and next to no power when we are with another group of people.

In this book, however, I am not primarily interested in power as leverage, or a means of self-determination and individualism. Yes, I argue that we can learn to use our loneliness as a source of personal empowerment, but the power that makes us strong in our loneliness is not really our power. It is the power of God through us and it is therefore a hidden power we cannot simply claim when we find it. Rather, we must learn to live in it. I therefore write this book because I am interested in the power of one that is available only as a gift and always only because we make ourselves available to receiving it.

Being available to God is not as easy as it sounds. If it were, I would never have felt the desire to write a book where I try to figure out how we make our loneliness available to God and thereby make ourselves available for the power of God. With that, I invite you to explore *The Power of One*.

ONE

Romantic Loneliness and the Creation of Human Beings

"IN THE BEGINNING GOD created the heavens and the earth."[1] We get no warning, no anticipation, no setting of the stage. Only a plain and direct announcement of the beginning. We do not know why God decided to create, and we have no access to the world behind the curtains of this very first beginning. For reflective creatures like ourselves, this is an almost unacceptable situation, and we keep banging our questions up against this back wall of the universe. Why? Why did God create the universe? What is the purpose of it all? Or, as the philosophers ask: Why is there anything at all and not nothing? And why can we not get an answer?

Martin Luther apparently listened to a lot of questions like these and finally responded in a way that probably silenced his audience. His "answer was that God was cutting sticks to cane people who ask such idle questions."[2] Obviously, this is not an answer at all, but that was undoubtedly his point. There is no answer. Yet, even if we listen to Luther and stop asking those questions, our silence is unlikely to last very long. There is something intensely appealing about hidden reasons behind the things we see but do not understand. We want to find those reasons, and we are frustrated when the beginning of things is as far as we are allowed to go back.

So, we settle and tell ourselves that the next best thing to knowing about the way things were *before* the beginning is knowing about the way things were *in* the beginning. The creation story is what takes us there. Generally, this story invites us to pursue two areas of inquiry, the origin of the cosmos and the origin of human beings. First, did the cosmos begin exclusively because of God's act of creation? Was it a big bang, followed by an evolutionary process? Or, was it perhaps a mix of divine creation and natural evolution? Second, what about the origin of human beings? When we pursue this line of inquiry, we enter the field of theological anthropology because we want to know about the significance of God's involvement in human life. We ask questions like this: How significant is it that God created human beings of two sexes? How much of our well-being depends on animals and the natural world? How does our relationship with God change after the fall? How does God speak to us? In this chapter, I am particularly interested in the creation story and what it tells us about the role of loneliness in romantic relationships between the two sexes.

Most people have a personal interest in romantic relationships. It seems natural for human beings to long for romantic love, and we all gravitate toward them to some degree. At the same time, it is just as natural to find ourselves struggling in those relationships when we have them. When romantic love becomes difficult, we start wondering where it started and this makes us go back to the beginning like nothing else. We want to get to the root of our struggle because we assume it can help us understand what is happening.

So, you must answer questions about your beginning. Does your childhood determine your choice of romantic partner? Did you fall for that man because he reminds you of your father? Do you remain single because the relationships of your childhood did not feel safe and now you stay away from intimate relationships? Is your infatuation with this woman a way for you to reconnect with your mother? It is the good fortune of the therapeutic industry that we are so committed to the idea that the beginning determines what will happen in the future.

Add to this that a romantic relationship has an almost unparalleled ability to make us feel less lonely. When attraction draws you to another person and the two of you settle in next to each other, it dispels your feelings of loneliness. You feel the pull of intimacy and imagine that an exclusive connection with this person will diminish the loneliness you either have or fear. Often, you have no eye for the possibility that this relationship could in fact increase your loneliness in the long run. What makes you pursue a romantic relationship can definitely be love, but it can also be the prospect of no longer being lonely.

But why does romantic attraction rank so highly on the scale of effective ways for us to heal our loneliness? Psychologists answer these questions by pointing us to the beginnings of our relationships, our lives, or our families. Theologians appreciate this but also point us to an earlier beginning, namely the one we hear about in the biblical story of creation. Especially the portion of this story that describes the relationship between Adam and Eve. We all know theirs is a subtle drama of cosmic consequences. But maybe we should stop and consider the possibility that it may also be the most important story in the Judeo-Christian tradition when it comes to the mystery of human loneliness.

The story of Adam and Eve is drama, but not necessarily a romantic one. They needed no personality tests to determine whether or not they were a good match. There was no competition between potential partners, and they did not pursue each other. Their relationship was never in question, and they never contemplated life without each other. They were just there, together, and did not relate to each other with the intensity of romantic attraction we know from our own lives. But, if their relationship was not a romantic one, what kind of relationship was it?

Maybe it was about a much more fundamental human need for interaction with the other sex—a need that makes romantic attraction seem like a much too narrow description of the reason we gravitate toward each other. I think about the story of Adam and Eve this way. Plus, I think their story encourages us to accept the idea that our relationship with the other sex defines who we are as *individual* persons in our own right. That is, when I contemplate the way they interacted, it looks like they needed to encounter and interact with the opposite sex in order to discover who they were on their own and apart from each other. This may apply to us in the following way. If you want to be the man God created you to be, you cannot ignore the importance of women in your life. Likewise, if you want to be the woman God created you to be, you cannot ignore the importance of men in your life.

Theologians from the modern period used to make this point when they argued that sexual difference is a theologically significant aspect of anthropology. Even though their argument is no longer as fashionable, I rely on it because it speaks to the aspects of Adam and Eve's story that I am interested in here. These theologians said "the encounter between man and woman—each sex being a distinct yet related mode of being human—is a relationship for which every human being must account as he or she responds to God."[3] This is to say that we are unable to enjoy human relationships if we disregard the difference between man and woman. God created human beings of two sexes, which makes sexual difference a fundamental condition of human life. In other words, we can only understand ourselves individually if we explore relationships with the opposite sex. They do not have to be romantic relationships, but they must involve full awareness of our sexual differences. This is the argument of these theologians and we must keep it in mind as we reflect on the role of loneliness in the relationship between man and woman.

So, if we look at our romantic relationships today, I think we underestimate how much and how often they are shaped by experiences of loneliness. Like nothing else, it is loneliness that makes the two sexes gravitate toward each other and that determines how we interact. Looking at the obvious ways this plays itself out, because we think a romantic relationship can make us less lonely, I find it curious that theologians do not pay more direct attention to the role of loneliness in the story of Adam and Eve. If we want to rely on the relationship between this first couple as a model by which we can understand our own relationships, we should pay some attention to the role of loneliness in their experiences with each other.

Let us do that by first looking at the Fall. Past this point, Adam and Eve were no longer allowed to live in the Garden of Eden, and all their relationships changed. They began to feel alienated and disconnected, from each other, the land, the animals, the natural world, and from God. They now lived with a nagging feeling that something was wrong with all kinds of things. They no longer felt at home in the world or in their own bodies. It was impossible for them to return to their first home in the Garden, and they had a difficult time navigating their new home outside the Garden.

Added to this fundamental sense of disconnect, interaction became more hierarchical. God spoke down to them. Man spoke down to woman, and, as the human population grew, they all started speaking down to each other. Animals and the natural world, too, became part of this game of subjection. They preyed on each other and were either domesticated or chased by humans. A new experience of rejection was beginning to circulate. Adam, Eve, and their growing family were now haunted by feelings of not fitting in and of not belonging. They were fighting over land and dominion, became distant from each other, and developed a craving for control. Everything because they now lived with a whole new premise of interaction: the loneliness of alienation. We call that sin.

I wonder if this loneliness might not have given a whole new quality to the relationship between Adam and Eve. What I have in mind is the intensity of attraction that we know from our own experiences with romantic relationships. Or the feelings that we will find personal fulfillment in an exclusive intimate connection with one special person who has become the object of our desire. We were not sure how to describe the relationship between Adam and Eve before the Fall, because it did not have the intensity we know from our own relationships. But, although we do not hear much about the way they interact after the Fall, I wonder if it did not have some of that intensity because it now involved loneliness. I think it did, and venture to make the assumption that the attraction we often experience in our romantic relationships gets much of its intensity from the loneliness that entered the relationship between the sexes at the Fall.

Why add anything to this point? The logic is simple. Adam and Eve fell, and therefore loneliness became an issue in their relationship and in all relationships to follow. Or maybe the logic is a little more complex, because we are still not entirely clear about the role of loneliness in the relationship between Adam and Eve *before* the Fall. The reason for this is one particular comment that God made after he had created Adam, before he had created Eve, and well in advance of their Fall. He said this: "It is not good that the man should be alone."[4] If we assume that loneliness became a problem only after the Fall, which we already did, then it is puzzling that Adam should have an experience of loneliness before the Fall. This could mean that God originally created human beings with the capacity to be lonely and then it is wrong to say that loneliness is something that entered the world with the Fall. Another variation of this point is to say that God first created Adam with no intention of also creating Eve, but then changed his mind when he realized Adam had a problem with loneliness.

Whatever the meaning of God's comment, I believe trying to understand it can give us important insights about the role loneliness plays in the relationship between the sexes. As we apply these insights, I believe they can help us articulate what it is reasonable to expect from romantic relationships. We tend to think they can heal our loneliness, and maybe God did have that purpose in mind when he first created Adam and Eve. But maybe the situation is a little more complex than that.

In the next two sections, I want to explore two options in this regard and then I invite you to make up your own mind. The first section argues that romantic relationships cannot, and are not designed to, heal loneliness. The second section argues the opposite, that God in fact did intend them to heal loneliness. Come along and see what you think, but be warned that these sections will stretch your mind. Both start with God's puzzling comment, "It is not good that the man should be alone,"[5] but arrive at opposite conclusions.

NOT TRUE: MARRIAGE HEALS ROMANTIC LONELINESS

Many people are lonely in their marriages. I know one couple who divorced after thirty years. Some months after the divorce was final, the woman started telling me about the loneliness in their marriage. It had slowly intensified over the years as her hopes for their relationship were disappointed. She had entered the marriage deeply in love with her husband, but, in the end, she knew she would not have survived if she had stayed in it. The relationship had become a prison of isolation. Today, several years after the divorce, she still speaks of her ex-husband as the man of her life, and she doubts she will marry again. "You can only love once," she says, and sometimes thinks it would have been easier if her husband had died. Then losing him would have been less about the loneliness of disappointed hopes, and more about the loneliness of untimely death.

The man remarried very soon after their divorce, but he does not talk about the way he met his second wife. A few months after his first wife moved out, another woman just sort of appeared. Today, they are happy in their new marriage, but when I asked him how they met, he refused to answer. "That is too personal," he said. During one of my conversations with him, he admitted he did not want to live without a wife and his reasoning behind remarriage was as simple as this: "I cannot live alone." He did not look up from the newspaper as he said this.

Reflecting on my conversations with this divorced couple, about their marriage relationship, I keep returning to the topic of romantic loneliness. They have tackled their loneliness differently, but both of them have struggled with it. The woman talks openly about it, perhaps because she is still dealing with it. Apart from that one comment, "I cannot live alone," I have not heard the man talk about it. He will discuss the romantic loneliness of other people, but does not like to talk about his own. He seems to consider the problem solved by his new marriage.

Can we conclude from this story, and from many more like it, that God did not design marriage to heal loneliness, and that we should therefore not expect that kind of healing from marriage? No. We cannot simply look at the marriages we have and then assume that they reveal God's intention for marriage. Sure, we can observe that married couples usually come to a point in their relationship where they must realize that having a partner does not make their loneliness go away. But this does not answer the question of whether or not God first created human beings with the capacity to be lonely, and then gave them to each other as a solution to loneliness. So, let us think again, and let us start by going back to God's puzzling comment that it was not good for the first human being to be alone.

Apparently, something about Adam being alone did not work, and God wanted to do something about it. This is odd, because why would God assess Adam's situation and find something wrong with it at this point? It was before the fall and everything should still be fine. If "God saw every thing that he had made, and indeed, it was very good,"[6] then there should be no reason for him to spot Adam's aloneness and say that it was "not good." To make matters worse, God's comment is also problematic because it makes us think of the two sexes as a hierarchy. If God created Eve because it was not good for Adam to be alone, then it makes her look like an afterthought in God's mind. It places her second in relation to Adam, and it gives the impression that God designed woman for the sake of man and as something like a human patch on his lonely heart. Or it makes her look like God's rescue act for the purpose of Adam's well-being. A gift from God that we might best describe as a precaution against the ache of loneliness that would otherwise make Adam miserable.[7]

Thinking about my friends, the divorced couple, it is hard not to notice a parallel. The man's quick response to the loneliness of divorce was to bring another woman into his life. In the beginning of this new relationship, it was difficult to tell why his partner had to be *this* particular woman, not just *a* woman. He could not avoid giving the impression that she functioned like a human patch on his otherwise lonely heart. All is now well and he and his new wife are happy together. Just as Adam and Eve were happy after they were both created and had met each other. Although Eve was created second, we have no reason to think that she was not as complete and unique as Adam. Plus, it is most likely that she would have been lonely for a partner too, had Adam not come into her life. Because she must have needed him as much as he needed her, one could easily argue that the order in which the two were created is of little, if any, significance. Still, this does not remove the impression that God was less intentional about Eve than about Adam.

If this impression causes us to wonder whether or not there was a hierarchy between man and woman before the fall, we need not doubt their relationship was hierarchical after the fall. When Adam and Eve had to start living outside the Garden of Eden, they no longer related to each other as equals. God spoke directly to this as they were leaving and gave Eve the following warning about her future life with Adam: "your desire shall be for your husband, and he shall rule over you."[8] God foresaw that Adam would tend to be in charge and that Eve would be drawn under his rule by a desire within herself. I think many of us have nodded in recognition of this warning as quite an accurate description of dynamics that tend to complicate our romantic relationships. How often do we find ourselves having relationship problems because we navigate each other as if man were above woman and woman below man?

Again, I see an example of this when I look at the couple whose marriage ended after thirty years. Over the course of three decades, they became increasingly isolated from each other because a hierarchy built up between them. The woman's desire for her husband became more and more enabling of his rule over her. She subjected herself to him, and he took that as an invitation to place her hierarchically below himself. In turn, the man's rule over his wife caused her to resist him more and more. He made decisions on her behalf, and she took that as an invitation to think of herself as inferior to him. These dynamics made good communication very difficult and each of them reinforced in the other person what eventually split them apart.

This is not to say they did not love each other. She genuinely loved him and did everything she could to understand him, to help him through difficult life seasons, and to support him in his professional work. Unfortunately, her desire to please him was very strong and it entered the mix in such a way that she had a difficult time acting without his permission. He genuinely loved her, too, and wanted to give her everything she needed and desired. Unfortunately, he did not realize that the things he gave her were not always the things she needed, and this made it difficult for her to express her true needs freely. When their marriage finally ended, her desire for him and his rule over her had drained their relationship of the intimacy and communication that could have brought them together. Their love for each other was not enough to keep them together.

This last point is important for our reflection on the relationship between the two sexes. It indicates that a marriage, or romantic relationship, does not only depend on love but just as much on the social aspect of communication and life together. This is why I suggest turning our attention away from God's puzzling comment about Adam's aloneness and, for a moment, focusing on something else. I want us to look at the implications of another brief comment that God made as he created human beings. Leading right up to the act, he said: "Let us make humankind in our image, according to our likeness."[9] This piece of information may turn out to be as, if not more, important as the one about Adam's aloneness when we want to understand the role of loneliness in his relationship to Eve. Wanting to know whether or not God created Eve second to Adam, it makes a difference to know that God had social humans beings in mind before he discovered Adam's loneliness. Because then we have an indication that God did in fact intend to create Eve before he created Adam. It would not make sense to say that God first planned the creation of social human beings, and then proceeded to be surprised when loneliness was a problem for the first one.

This means that if God wanted to create human beings in the image of a divine "us," then he must have intended for Adam and Eve to be as intimately related as one divine being relates to (we assume) himself. And then we should never look at Adam or Eve in isolation because they only made sense together, and it was their relationship with each other that defined them individually. The man was not a man without the woman. Nor was the woman a woman without the man. We cannot say it was romantic attraction that brought them into contact with each other. Rather, they were joined by a predetermined social connection even before they had a chance to know about each other, and long before they could possibly have awareness of their own relationship.

That God wanted human beings to be social, and then moved on to create the two sexes, makes me think of the relationship between man and woman as an engine of social energy. When we interact with each other, something happens to our sense of feeling connected. We start wondering about each other, we become curious and we begin to ask each other questions. I know many of us dislike the idea that the two sexes are different, and that there are things each does that the other does not. I also know many of us dislike the idea that the difference between the sexes is something we need from each other in order to be at our own best.

I think we should challenge these dislikes in ourselves and I think the impulse of curiosity about the opposite sex is important for our general sense of well-being. It makes us gravitate toward each other and it generates social energy. We thrive in each other's company. This gives meaning to the argument that connections with the opposite sex are necessary for a full experience of what it means to be human. If God created man and woman when he had social human beings in mind, then the connections between the sexes, and the curiosity they have about each other, must be the essential idea behind the design of human beings.

Let me be very clear about this one thing, though. I am not trying to argue that a marriage relationship is the only, or even the best, way to explore our curiosity about the opposite sex. It is just that marriage has some hot-spot characteristics that encourage curiosity between the sexes. In my observation, we have many other opportunities to explore each other across the sexes. It is just that, for some unfortunate reason, we often miss the opportunity to interact across the sexes in a meaningful way, or we simply disregard them. If you are a man, for instance, when was the last time you spent an afternoon in conversation with a woman who is thirty or forty years your senior? Or, if you are a mature woman, when was the last time you had lunch with a male college student who is craving to learn how women think?

For the sake of our topic, however, I want to stay focused on marriage as a hot-spot opportunity for the sexes to be social. More specifically, I want to think about the painful implication that if my marriage fails, then I will experience *myself* as a failure. It must be this way, because the intimate connection of marriage is an essential experience of what it means for me to be human. If this connection breaks, then it must also be an attack on the most essential part of my identity. It should therefore be no surprise that it makes me feel as if there is something wrong with me as a human being.

If you have read Daphne du Maurier's novel *Rebecca*, you may remember Mrs. De Winter, the heroine of the story. She went through a marriage experience that illustrates this point. To refresh our memory, let me paraphrase her story in a couple of sentences. She was young and infatuated with a wealthy widower, whom she married. Many ordeals later, it dawned on her that their marriage could not survive the way they related to each other, and this became a threat to her sense of identity. So much so that, throughout the story, readers are not even certain that Rebecca is a real person. Maybe she is only a ghost that keeps haunting her husband's manor. In any case, one of her most painful confessions about their unhappy marriage came in the form of her comment that "there was nothing quite so shaming, so degrading, as a marriage that had failed."[10] Their story ends when Manderley, their home, is going up in flames.

Mrs. De Winter is a fictional character, and definitely no biblical theologian, but her confession is right to the point of God's motivation for the creation of human beings. A failed marriage is an attack on the essence of what it means to be human and is therefore one of the most shameful and degrading experiences we can have. When something attacks the social connection between men and women, it also attacks human identity. It brings loneliness into our relationships.

The fact that our current divorce rates are as high as they are is no proof that we do not feel the pain of a failed marriage. We tend to think divorce is no longer as devastating as it used to be because it happens all the time and, today, hardly comes with any social stigma whatsoever. But, a high divorce rate only gives us the information that a high number of people carry the burden of a failed marriage. It does not tell us that the pain of divorce no longer affects us.[11]

The pain of a failed marriage makes us lonely. Perhaps even worse, our fear of a failed relationship holds us back from talking about loneliness when we experience it within marriage. Somehow marriage is like a label on our forehead that reads "I am not lonely," and therefore it requires a lot of courage for a married person to talk about personal loneliness. In this situation, marriage easily becomes a prison of isolation more than an opportunity to experience the fullness of being human. Loneliness in marriage can be so much more intense than loneliness as a single person.

The sexual intimacy of a marriage relationship is not immune to loneliness either. In fact, this is often the place where the sense of imprisonment becomes the strongest. William Hulme talks about it this way: "In spite of labels we attach to intercourse—be intimate, make love, come together—the act itself may be quite the opposite. Sex may be exploited to achieve selfish satisfaction. Then it is a substitute for intimacy rather than its expression."[12] We tend to think of selfish satisfaction as a deliberate choice to harm someone else, or we think of it as abuse, but sexual satisfaction need not be those things in order to be selfish. A lack of concern for the well-being of our spouse is enough to make us selfish. If we disregard the need to care for him or her, then we create the kind of distance that sets the game of hierarchical interaction in motion. We already talked about that. In that situation, sex itself becomes a substitute for the intimacy it could give us. It becomes another way of holding our partner hostage to our selfishness. How painful and how lonely that we should seek sexual intimacy with another person, only to find ourselves walking away from the experience all disappointed and lonely.

So, what kind of clarity do all these things give us on the question of whether or not God designed marriage to heal romantic loneliness? Two things. First, the loneliness of a failed marriage, as well as the loneliness within marriage, is so intensely painful because it threatens what it means to be human. It attacks the social connections we naturally have between the sexes and that marriage invites us to explore. Second, love, romance, and the sexual intimacy of marriage are no free tickets to an experience of the fullness of what it means to be human. Marriage only becomes that kind of experience when it *also* involves the social connection God created man and woman to have.

The couple that divorced after thirty years knew this firsthand. As hard as they tried, they could not seem to benefit from the connection that was there for them to have. They were attracted to each other, fell in love, and loved each other through the years. Whether or not their attraction first developed because they hoped a relationship would heal their loneliness, I am in no place to determine. It is clear, however, that whatever hopes they might have had, the experience of loneliness and isolation was like a permanent infection in their relationship. The love, the romance, and the sexual intimacy they shared did not survive their lack of a solid social connection.

As this couple therefore illustrates, loneliness so often replaces the social connection God created man and woman to have with each other. When this happens, I argue, it somehow confuses us and we start to think that if only our love, our romance, or our sexual intimacy were more fulfilling, then loneliness would not be our problem. This is where loneliness starts to fuel the intensity of our romantic feelings for each other. The lonelier we are, the more hopeful we can become that a partner will be the answer to our problem of loneliness.

Making matters worse, we then add another layer of confusion to this thinking when we read the creation story and conclude that God gave Eve to Adam as a solution to his problem of loneliness. To this, I say: God did not. His original intent was to create the two sexes around the experience of a natural social connection. Not that they should be a solution to each other's loneliness.

This conclusion, however, requires that we understand Adam's first encounter with aloneness as something positive. The next section suggests how we can do that. It makes the argument that aloneness is something positive that we bring with us into our marriage relationships and that marriage, in turn, makes us more comfortable with ourselves as individuals. I therefore invite you to read along. If the next section convinces you that Adam's aloneness is a good thing, then you can return to the section I now bring to a close, and then you may agree with the following conclusion.

Marriage does not heal loneliness, because God did not design it for that purpose. What does heal loneliness is the social connection men and women are wired by God to develop in each other's company. Yes, marriage is one place where we often succeed in developing that social connection, but it is not the only place. Nor is this connection guaranteed by marriage.

TRUE: MARRIAGE HEALS ROMANTIC LONELINESS

If marriage is not designed to heal loneliness, then why do so many people still experience that it actually does so? Why do married persons say it changed their lives to have someone permanently by their side? And, why do single persons desire marriage? Or, why do celibate nuns and monks fall in love?

I know we already read the story of Adam and Eve. Even so, I suggest reading it again, only this time from the perspective of what I think are some of John Paul II's most intriguing insights about the intimacy Adam and Eve shared with each other. More specifically, I want to focus on his argument that the first human being, Adam, brought the experience of "being alone" into an intimate relationship with Eve.

If we apply John Paul II's argument to our own marriages, then we have good reasons to think an intimate relationship is not primarily about a relationship with someone else. It is just as much about being aware of oneself as a separate individual. Then marriage is not only about being together, but also about being comfortable in one's own individual being. And here is the question I think this raises: If spousal intimacy can make us more comfortable as individuals, does it not also protect us against the experience of loneliness? I will argue that it does.

In my opinion, John Paul II's argumentative style can be a little on the philosophically sophisticated side. Real life experiences with romantic relationships are often more complex than his ideal descriptions of marriage tend to convey. This, of course, gives no license to dismiss them. It only means we have to think about ways in which we can apply such ideals to real life.

Therefore, I want to start this section by introducing you to the real life experience of a married couple, a single man, and a celibate monk. In fact, it was their comments about intimate relationships that first stimulated my interest in the possibility that spousal intimacy can increase our sense of individual identity. And that thereby it decreases our loneliness. Their comments made me curious about John Paul II's ideal views of marriage and caused me to think they might be of more practical value than one might think at first.

Let me start with the married couple, Laura and Bob. We find their story in a book about intimacy. They give an interview where they tell us it changed their lives when they found each other. They describe their intimacy as the most important aspect of their relationship, but also say that intimacy is not a goal in and of itself. The most interesting change they experienced was unexpected and not about their own relationship. First, this is how they explain intimacy as something that gives each of them courage, security, and confidence: "We have no doubts, no fears . . . in an odd way, we are one unit—two parts fused into one."[13] Next, the interview moves on to the unexpected and perhaps most powerful part of their story. Here is Bob's brief explanation of his new sense of self and a growing appreciation of others:

> Until I met Laura, I hardly ever felt comfortable or unstrained with other people—or with myself. I don't think I understood myself very well; I didn't accept myself and I didn't really care about other people the way I do now.[14]

It is hard to imagine a better description of the positive change an intimate relationship can bring to a person's basic sense of being in the world. This man's focus is not on the relationship he has with his wife, but about the way relating to her has changed him as an individual person. In relation to others, not in relationship to her. She entered his life and somehow became the facilitator of a stronger sense of social connection. Before meeting his wife, he felt alienated from other people. After meeting her, feelings of alienation and estrangement no longer dominated his other relationships.

Now consider Donald Miller, a single man and writer. I read his spiritual memoirs for pleasure and do not expect him to deal with heavy theological issues. Nonetheless, he makes an interesting comment about the marriage he desires for himself, and there is no mistaking its theological significance. His hope is that marriage will help him develop a stronger sense of being alone. In his words: "I want to marry a girl who, when I am with her, makes me feel alone."[15] Notice that he does not want to marry someone who makes him feel lonely, but someone who makes him feel alone. His comments are brief, but he explains his desire this way: "I guess what I am saying is, I want to marry a girl whom I feel completely comfortable with, comfortable being myself."[16]

You would think a single man knows what it means to be alone, but he is apparently talking about something other than merely being without company. It is not that he hopes for a wife who will give him permission to take time away for himself so he can enjoy not having people around. That would be the same as saying that the absence of his wife would give him a sense of being alone. No, he imagines that her presence, not her absence, will make him feel alone. In other words, his desire for spousal intimacy is connected to his desire to be comfortable being himself.

Finally, consider Thomas Merton, a Trappist monk and a prolific writer. He spent several years as a hermit, living in an isolated cottage in the woods. Part of his commitment as a monk was to live a celibate life, remain unmarried, and abstain from sexual intimacy and activity. Interestingly, this was not enough to keep him from meeting a woman, falling in love with her, and developing a deeply intimate relationship with her.

Merton wrote about their love in his journals and expressed considerable awareness of his desire for spousal intimacy. He could not control this desire and was quite certain it was rooted in, as he says, a "persistent desire to be somebody."[17] Interestingly, he thought the appeal of romantic intimacy was hidden underneath his desire for a sense of personal identity. Also, he did not think falling in love was a sudden and stand-alone phenomenon for him. Rather, he said, "I think really it all comes from roots that had simply lain dormant since I entered the monastery."[18] In spite of his genuine commitment not to be ruled by the longing for a woman, he was hooked by it when she showed up and became for him a promise of personal identity.

Merton never expressed any regret about the vow of celibacy. Nor did he and M. consummate their love relationship sexually. Yet, their intimacy changed him and gave him a strong feeling of being real. In his own words, "I feel less real, somehow, without our constant communication, our sense of being in communion."[19] What we have here is a celibate man who was surprised by the power of intimacy. Not because he had no idea what it was, but because "really, instead of being all wrong, it seemed eminently right. We now love with our whole bodies anyway, and I have the complete feel of her being (except her sex) as completely me."[20] The power of intimacy was seemingly as strong a force in his life as it was in the lives of Laura and Bob, the married couple.

We now have three examples of individuals who live in very different relationship situations and yet, all of them relate intimacy to the experience of becoming more secure in their identity as individual persons. Of course, we cannot make theological conclusions based on their comments and personal experiences. But, if we turn to the story of Adam and Eve, and if we rely on John Paul II's reflections on their relationship, it looks like their intimacy had some of the same quality as we have seen in our three examples.

John Paul II's argument focuses on Adam's aloneness and being without a companion at first. The story of how Adam then met Eve illustrates how "the meaning of original solitude enters and becomes part of the meaning of original unity."[21] In less sophisticated language, this is to say that the first human being's experience of aloneness became an important part of the relationship Adam and Eve developed later. In even plainer language, and if we apply it to marriage in general, this means that marriage is just as much about our sense of individual identity as it is about becoming one with another person.

Apparently, John Paul II thinks we need to revise our common understanding of God's comment that it was not good for Adam to be alone. He wants us to see that this comment marks an important point in God's process of creating human beings. The thing to notice is John Paul II's emphasis on the creation process. He argues that God created man and woman in a double act of creation, and that the comment about Adam's aloneness marks the transition between the two. First, God created one human being, and then—by putting that one to sleep—he pressed the reset button and started creating all over again, this time a male and a female human being.

If I were to use a metaphorical illustration of this process, I would compare God's double act of creation to the work it takes to push a car out of a snow bank. Your first push gets the car going and creates the beginning of an exit track. Then you let it glide back behind the beginning point so you can give it another hard push. This push sends the car over the hump and releases it from the snow. I think of the first push as God's act of creating the first human being, and I think of the second push as God's act of creating man and woman. The two make one complete act of creation, but they are still separate.

It is in the first creation story that God announces he will create human beings in his own image and that they will be of two sexes, male and female.[22] With this plan in mind, God creates them in one single act of creation.[23] It is as simple as that. The idea of man and woman leads directly to the creation of man and woman.

In contrast, the second creation story leaves us with the impression that there was a first human being and that this person was both alone and unsexed. Not sexless, but just not identified as any particular sex. It is important for John Paul II to emphasize that the text of the second creation story does not identify the first human being as a male person. Rather, it uses the Hebrew word Adam, in its meaning of "human being," not "male human being." This is significant because it is only in the second creation story that God notices that Adam, the first human being, is alone. So, apparently, the aloneness God identifies in Adam is not the aloneness of the first male but the aloneness of the first (unsexed) human being.

In any case, John Paul II is intrigued by the second creation story. He thinks it contains some insights about individual human development that we do well not to miss. To this end, we must pay some focused attention to Adam's personal development before the time when God created Eve. This development has to do with all the animals. When God noticed Adam was alone, he "formed every animal of the field and every bird of the air, and brought them to the man to see what he would call them."[24] We often think of this as a situation where Adam, somewhat desperately, searched for a helper among the animals, without finding one. John Paul II does not reject this reading, but wants us to notice something else: namely that Adam walked away from interaction with all the animals and had become a different being. Not different as in "Adam is no longer human," but different as in "Adam now knows what it means to be human and what it means to be different from all the other creatures."

God did make the comment that he wanted Adam to look for a partner among the animals, but Adam did not seem to have that same intention. All the animals just kept coming at him, one after another, and Adam responded to them by noticing what they were and giving them a name. So, if we look at the situation from Adam's perspective, giving names to all the animals was no deliberate search for a partner. Rather, in Adam, John Paul II sees a person who had been roaming the earth for a sense of self, and who could finally stop that search when all the animals had names. At that point, Adam was astutely aware of one new thing: "I am alone! I am the only one of my kind. All other creatures are not human. Only I am human." God already knew this, which is what he communicated when he commented on Adam's aloneness, but now Adam knew it, too.

This is important to John Paul II because it means that Adam's new knowledge was also a new *kind* of knowledge. It was self-knowledge, or what we might describe as self-consciousness, or self-awareness. It gave Adam a sense of personal identity. There was no way Adam could have had this kind of knowledge before going through the long process of identifying all the other kinds of creatures. Nor was this self-knowledge something God could just give to Adam because then it would not have been Adam's own.[25] The very definition of self-knowledge means that absolutely no one, other than oneself, can develop knowledge of self. Otherwise it would not possibly be knowledge of oneself. Hence, giving names to all the animals was a process of self-discovery where Adam developed knowledge of what it means to be alone. It is this whole process God identifies in that one comment about Adam's aloneness. John Paul II calls Adam's aloneness *original solitude*.

This takes us from the first to the second of God's two acts of creating human beings. That is, God took Adam's new knowledge as a signal that the first human being was now complete, and then he reset the creation process by putting Adam to sleep. John Paul II thinks of this as God's way of returning "to the moment before creation, *in order that the solitary 'man' may by God's creative initiative reemerge from that moment in his double unity as male and female*."[26] This is a packed comment that challenges us to think about the first human being as solitary and alone, but also as a representation of both male and female. Because John Paul

II thinks of Adam as neither male nor female, he also discourages us from thinking that one sex was superior to the other because it was created first. His point is that the text does not allow us to distinguish between male and female until after Adam reawakened from sleep. Rather, we should think of the two as a unity from the very beginning. They were neither separate, nor distinct, until God brought two physically separate bodies out of Adam's one body.[27]

We can now see what John Paul II means by saying that aloneness was an important part of Adam and Eve's relationship. The first two human beings simply could not become one unit without first being aware of themselves and secure in their own identity as individuals. When they looked at each other the first time, then they had already looked at themselves first and knew this: "I am a human being. Distinct from all other creatures." It would have been impossible for them to form a unity of two human beings if they did not have this knowledge first.

Why does this matter when we think about Laura and Bob, Donald Miller, and Thomas Merton? They all talked about spousal intimacy as something that makes us more secure as separate individual beings. But is that what John Paul II says happened for Adam and Eve? Not yet. So far, he has only argued that they were secure in their individuality *before* they became a unity of two. Next, however, he does move on to say that Adam and Eve found individual identity as a consequence of first experiencing an intimate unity with each other. He does this by pointing out that it was because they first discovered each other that they could discover themselves individually.

Think about the time Adam and Eve encountered each other the first time. The text of the second creation story says it was after this first encounter that they became one flesh. What they saw in each other was not the possibility of a unity but someone exactly like themselves. They were a reflection of each other. In that moment, they both looked at another person who was alone, who had self-knowledge, and who knew what it means to be human. Adam saw himself in Eve, and Eve saw herself in Adam. In John Paul II's words they were the first to experience that "the search for the human identity of the one who, at the beginning, is 'alone,' must always pass through . . . 'communion.'"[28] Since then, this has been the experience of all other couples. So, John Paul II now argues that being intimately together as a couple is an opportunity for each of the two individual persons to discover himself as a man, or herself as a woman.

Which is another way of saying that it is through our experience of unity that we become comfortable with ourselves as individuals.

Applying this to the experience of our married couple, single man, and celibate monk, we now see how their experiences affirm John Paul II's argument. They were individual, self-aware beings before they entered an intimate romantic relationship.[29] But the intimacy they experienced, and the unity they formed with their partner, was a catalyst for each of them in their individual and personal development. It strengthened their sense of individual identity, and becoming one with another person made them more aware of themselves.

For Laura and Bob it meant becoming more confident and secure in the company of other people. For Donald Miller it means hoping to marry a woman who will make him feel more comfortable with himself exactly as he is. For Thomas Merton it meant the fulfillment of his desire to be more real and to gain a sense of being "someone." In all three examples, we are looking at individual persons who develop a stronger sense of themselves as a result of their sense of communion and unity with another person.

We are now at a point where we can indeed conclude that marriage heals romantic loneliness. If we accept John Paul II's reading of the story of Adam and Eve, we see that, originally, God designed spousal unity to increase our level of comfort with ourselves. God orchestrated the encounter between Adam and Eve in such a way that their partnership with each other made them comfortable with themselves. The partnership of marriage thus has the power to turn our sense of loneliness into a sense of comfort with ourselves. It gives us the opportunity to change loneliness into solitude. Marriage can make us comfortable with ourselves, and it can drive away the discomfort of loneliness we feel when we are alienated from ourselves and from others.

TWO

Spiritual Loneliness and Redemption in Christ

SPIRITUAL LONELINESS IS THE experience of God's absence, or feeling separated from God. It is the sense that we have lost a connection with God, even if this loss only amounts to an unfulfilled desire to know God. It can manifest as a quiet longing for God, or a deeper personal desire to belong to Jesus. In its different manifestations, I think of it as rooted in the kind of loneliness St. Augustine described as an internal restlessness that only God can calm: "Our heart is restless until it rests in you."[1] We may not be able to articulate our own desire for God, but when we find rest in him, we know it was the thing we desired all along.

What I call spiritual loneliness, some researchers describe as *cosmic* or *existential loneliness*. Thinking about loneliness as cosmic effectively invokes the image of a vast universe where we can find no place that gives us a sense of belonging. It suggests that no matter how far we travel in the universe, we cannot find the kind of rest St. Augustine talked about. If we use the term existential, it more effectively portrays spiritual loneliness as a personal sense of feeling lost because we want to find God but cannot. It gets at the unsettling experience of disorientation it creates to know that God exists but somehow we cannot find him.

In conversations about spiritual loneliness, people often ask me why it is not another word for depression. This is a difficult question to answer because the two often come as a packaged deal. Still, although the difference is subtle, it is significant. When we have a fulfilling experience of God's presence, then we do not feel spiritually lonely. This is likely to give us a sense of psychological well-being. Yet, not feeling spiritually lonely is no guarantee against depression. The reverse is true too: lacking an experience of God's presence can, but does not necessarily, cause depression. All of this means that just because spiritual loneliness and depression are often related, it does not mean that they have to be related or always will be. We can have depressions and at the same time have real experiences of God's presence. Just as we do not have to become depressed because we never experienced God's presence.

Others want to know why spiritual loneliness is not another word for hopelessness and despair. This, too, is a difficult question to answer, because spiritual loneliness often makes us think the future does not hold good things for us. Despair means losing hope, and if we do not think there is a God who cares, then we are likely to have a more difficult time hoping in things we cannot see yet. The tricky thing about despair, however, is that it always implies some measure of resistance against hope. A resistance we deliberately create.[2] We rarely make deliberate or definitive decisions that hope is not for us. But we do make little, seemingly insignificant, conclusions against hope that, if we do not nip them in the bud, slowly add up and grow into a more pervasive sense of despair. Spiritual loneliness does not need this element of choice in order to develop, because it is much too dependent on God's initiative. Yes, choosing to believe that God can be present in our lives makes spiritual loneliness less likely, but whether or not God actually will be present depends more on God than it depends on us.

Hence, even though spiritual loneliness often belongs in the company of both depression and despair, it still has a distinctly different quality. Whether we experience God's presence depends on God actually making himself present much more than it depends on our psychology and choice for or against hope. For this reason, I argue that we mostly experience spiritual loneliness as something painful that is imposed upon us. I claim that we are, to a large extent, powerless against spiritual loneliness because we do not have the power to make God present. We can invoke and pursue God, but we cannot decide if, or when, he will manifest.

I now venture to claim that this element of powerlessness makes spiritual loneliness a matter of suffering. More precisely, it is my claim that we tend to experience spiritual loneliness as something God could remove but—for reasons we cannot figure out—chooses not to remove. When we know God has the power to manifest in our lives, and we do what we can to connect with him, and it does not happen, then how can we not experience his absence as imposed? It is as if God is hiding, or is making it impossible for us to find him. This is what I mean by saying that spiritual loneliness is a matter of suffering.

So, by suffering I do not mean pain. Pain can be physical, as it is when we are seriously ill, abused, or find ourselves in an accident, for example. Or it can be psychological, as when we are neglected as children, misrepresented as adults, or become victims of injustice. Pain can also be the result of things like cultural, mental, or financial stresses. In all these instances, however, we have some level of understanding of why we are hurting, and therefore we do not as easily think of it as suffering. This was the observation Eric Cassell made about patients in the medical world. He said, "Patients can writhe in pain from kidney stones and by their own admission not be suffering, because they 'know what it is'; they may also report considerable suffering from apparently minor discomfort when they do not know its source."[3] It is not that we desire pain or think it is acceptable when it comes. It is just that because we know the cause of it, we can make logical sense of it, and then we tend not to think of it as a matter of suffering. The more incomprehensible the pain, the more suffering it implies.

In my reading of this definition, we also begin to ask spiritual questions when our pain turns into suffering. Suffering is a deeper experience than pain because it involves asking questions about God's willingness to help and protect us. When pain turns into suffering, we no longer understand why we have to hurt, and we may contemplate the possibility that God lacks willingness to help and protect us. This robs us of the confidence that God is on our side, and we may develop a fear that this is a universe where we could never find a sense of belonging. We know only a move on God's part can restore our spiritual confidence when we are in this situation, and this is my reason to think of spiritual loneliness as suffering, not just pain.

With these reflections in mind, it is easy to see how spiritual loneliness can cause both depression and despair. Who, out of the suffering it implies to feel lost in a godless universe, would not be overcome by the awful feeling that life has little, if any, purpose? Spiritual loneliness is a terrifying kind of loneliness and it easily lands us in the midst of despairing thoughts like these: "It does not matter whether I live or die." "Why not just make an end of it all?" These are words of death, not of life, and they suggest that we must fear spiritual loneliness as much as we fear death itself.

In the Protestant theological tradition of St. Augustine, Martin Luther, and Søren Kierkegaard, the good news is that Christ saves us from this death of spiritual loneliness. It teaches us that Christ offers redemption and regeneration so we no longer have to be alienated from God. Broadly speaking, theologians of this tradition talk about redemption as a process of acknowledging and confessing one's sins, and then receiving forgiveness and regeneration in return. It is a personally transformative process and it restores our relationship with God. In that process, we may have to endure spiritual loneliness for a while, but only until we find relief from it because faith in Christ redeems us and lifts us out of it.

The Catholic tradition conceives of redemption a little differently. Here it is more intimately tied to our spiritual life journey and depends on whether or not we learn to suffer well over the long haul. It is about developing the virtue of patience through suffering more than about Christ lifting us out of suffering. Redemption works itself out within us as we embrace our suffering and learn to grow through it. In this tradition, the most effective way to protect ourselves against suffering is to refrain from questioning God's intentions merely because we do not understand why he lets us suffer. Rather, patiently and humbly accepting our suffering is how we disarm it, and when we do that we will discover that suffering becomes strangely bearable—even if it were to last a lifetime.[4]

To conclude this initial reflection on spiritual loneliness, I will say two things. First, we need to deal with it as a matter of suffering. Second, we can either approach spiritual loneliness with the generally Protestant hope that Christ will redeem us from it and lift us out of it. Or we can take a patient and more Catholic stance where we learn to suffer through it. I devote the next two sections to these options. The first section follows the Protestant line of thinking and arrives at the conclusion that redemption in Christ does not heal spiritual loneliness. The second section explores the Catholic approach and concludes that redemption in Christ in fact does heal spiritual loneliness. Which one of these approaches you find most convincing is a decision you need to make for yourself.

NOT TRUE: CHRIST HEALS SPIRITUAL LONELINESS

I was shocked the first time I heard someone say to me that he was suffering more than Jesus ever did. I remember the hospital room where it happened. The man in the bed was forty-two and a few weeks away from death. I was standing next to him and remember how the light streamed through the window, how the nurse was walking past the foot-end of the bed, and how the Saturday morning sounds of a busy city reached us through the hospital walls. He had been sweating all night and his temples showed musty green lines of verdigris running from just behind his eyes back to his ears. They were caused by the chemical reaction between his sweat and the frame of his glasses. He was my friend, but his face did not look like the face I knew. And then he said it. "Anette. I do not want you to see this. You must leave the room. My suffering is worse than Jesus' suffering." I do not know why, but I believed him. I believed his pain was worse than the pain Jesus experienced during his crucifixion. His words somehow transfixed me, and I could not leave the room. I am not sure he noticed that I stayed.

Suffering like this makes us lonely. Not so much because others would not understand us if we tried to share our experience with them. It is more that such intense suffering makes us feel that God is not with us, or that God is possibly even against us. It is this kind of loneliness that I call spiritual loneliness, and it reveals most clearly that loneliness is a matter of suffering. Whether we have to endure it first-hand, second-hand, or from a distance, it is a loneliness we all fear. It follows us through life, much like a dark cloud that threatens to descend upon us any time. We may not be aware of it, or we may deny it, but our fear of it is there.

How do we deal with this beast of spiritual loneliness? To answer this question, I suggest we broaden our perspective and think about the ways we can best deal with suffering in general. Doing this, two questions seem to impress themselves upon us with more urgency than others. First, how can God possibly be of help when suffering has become unbearable? Second, how can we receive God's help when suffering is unbearable? We want to know where we can find the help we need, and we want to know how we can benefit from it when we find it.

In recent times, there is probably no Protestant theologian who has thought about these questions more thoroughly than Jürgen Moltmann. His desire to understand how God suffers with us, even in our worst suffering, is hard to match. He is unusually committed to a theology that recognizes those whose suffering is simply "too much," without justification, and often ignored by society because they cannot make themselves heard. Although it would hardly be fair to think of Moltmann as a political theologian, his theology is very concerned with matters of social justice. What is more, the fact that he keeps returning to the writings of Elie Wiesel, Fyodor Dostoevsky, Albert Camus, and other existentialist writers is indication enough that we are dealing with a thinker who looks straight into the eyes of injustice, despair, and death itself. Moltmann is relentless. He wants Christian theology to be convincing enough for those who tell us they suffer more than Jesus ever did.

In his early work, Moltmann's response to such overwhelming suffering was a straightforward and simple message of hope. He wanted us to look at Jesus' resurrection and remember that his story ended in triumph. This, he said, is God's promise to us that we, too, are headed for a future of resurrection and triumph over evil where suffering will be no more. We know for certain this future will come because we know it already came to Jesus. Part of God's promise of resurrection is that the suffering we endure now is nothing compared to the triumph and the fulfillment we will enjoy when it is all over.

When I think back to the hospital room that Saturday morning, I saw a brief glimpse of Moltmann's resurrection hope in action. It happened when, unexpectedly, a little, older woman entered the room. I did not know her, but apparently she knew my dying friend. She showed up at the door, quickly evaluated the situation, walked up to the bed, leaned her head toward his ear and said, "Remember, the best is yet to come." He hardly noticed she had come to visit, and she definitely did not notice me. The situation was somehow too intense for those kinds of notices to be paid. But my friend looked at her and listened to her. Then she hesitated for a moment, looked around the room, said a few words of goodbye, turned toward the door, and left. The moment was almost over before it had begun. Moltmann would probably say that I remember her words so clearly because they carried the power of the hope of resurrection.

My friend died in the power of this hope. But those of us who continue to live, Moltmann says, should also be empowered by the hope of resurrection so that we can start changing the world into a better place. Hope is not only for the dying, it is also for the living. Christians are people of hope and are therefore also people of change, so we must get involved and be actively opposed to injustice and suffering before change can begin to happen. Things like prayer and sympathy are good, but not enough. Active opposition to any and all kinds of destructive power is a vital part of what it means to believe in the promise of resurrection.

I write these paragraphs two days after President Barack Obama's inauguration and I have to quote him because his message of hope could have come straight out of Moltmann's theology. On election night, the

President-elect said that those who had been told, for so long, to be fearful and doubtful could now finally "put their hands on the arc of history and bend it once more toward the hope of a better day." If you have heard Martin Luther King's famous "I have a dream speech" from 1963, you know Obama was making a reference to a particularly famous comment from that speech. Dr. King said, "The arc of the moral universe is long, but it bends toward justice."

Moltmann would agree with this way of thinking about history. Except, he would add that Christian believers are people of a particularly powerful hope that will culminate in the resurrection. It is when Christians actively oppose injustice that the arc of history starts bending toward the event of resurrection, which will be the final and ultimate manifestation of divine justice. In fact, he says, we might just as well accept that God has that particular good end in mind and will make it happen. And then we should get to work for the oppressed, against the oppressor.

As Moltmann has realized over time, however, there is something lacking about this message of hope. What first bothered him was the fact that some people must suffer so intensely that the promise of a better day to come simply does not match their suffering. There is something wrong with your economy of suffering and hope when you make the claim that future triumph is enough to make up for present suffering. Something is out of balance. Hope for the future does not comfort us sufficiently in the suffering we have to endure today. It gives some comfort, but not enough to match the worst kind of suffering.

Perhaps an even more perplexing thing about this unbalanced economy of suffering and hope is the situation where people die very young, in childhood, or in early infancy. Of course, as Moltmann says, "their fate can have great meaning for other people, but where and how will their own lives be completed?"[5] The reality of this observation suddenly struck me recently, when I read a little book entitled, *This Incomplete One*.[6] It is a collection of sermons given at funerals for children and young adults. It is true, I thought, that those whose lives are cut unreasonably short lose the most fundamental opportunity to become a person. How can they be complete persons when there is close to no life story for them to tell? Even the New Testament teaches us that all people need the opportunity to live in order to become complete. How else would it make sense to say that God, "who began a good work in you will carry it on to completion until the day of Christ Jesus?"[6] If God is in the business of "completing us" in

47

this life, then to start with birth, but to skip life itself and jump right into resurrection, makes little sense. The most important part is missing. It is the part where a person becomes a person.[7]

So, Moltmann had to get back to work in order to give an effective response to this imbalanced economy of suffering and hope. He needed more than the simple hope in a better day and a future of triumph. His efforts resulted in what is perhaps his best known book, *The Crucified God*. In it, Moltmann started urging us to pay more attention to Jesus' crucifixion than to his resurrection. Our hope should not build on how the story of Jesus ended, but on what happened before that end, during the time when Jesus suffered and died. The thing is this, Moltmann said. God is three persons who dwell mysteriously within each other, so whatever happens to one of the three happens to all three of them. This means that no part of God could have played it safe during the crucifixion by somehow escaping the impact of what was happening. That was the real drama of hope playing itself out. When Jesus was crucified and died, it was all of God who experienced crucifixion and death, not just part of God. God was crucified when Jesus was crucified.

To make his point clear, Moltmann used some rather dramatic words. He said that after the event of the crucifixion, "something new and strange . . . entered the metaphysical world."[8] It was as if the entire cosmos was caught in astonishment, holding its breath, and trying to accept the idea that God had taken the full blow of death. But why, he wanted to know, do we still hold our breath, and why do we still have such a hard time accepting this whole idea of a suffering God? Writing *The Crucified God* was his way to help us accept that God did indeed suffer and die.

This should be good news for those of us who have been shocked to realize that some people have to suffer more than Jesus ever did. It makes quite a difference to believe in a God who has proved himself ready to suffer crucifixion without trying to escape its full impact. This God is a trustworthy God. More than that, it is a God who is involved in the conditions of real human existence. True involvement requires willingness to sacrifice for the sake of others, and that is exactly what a suffering God does. He sacrifices for others. If we worshipped a God who had somehow escaped the impact of crucifixion, then we would worship a poor God. "For a God who is incapable of suffering is a being who cannot be involved."[9] God *is* capable of suffering, however, and God *is* involved. We know this because he has already proved it.[10]

48

When my dying friend therefore said he was suffering more than Jesus, I should have reminded him that there is more to Jesus' sufferings than what meets the eye. It was not just Jesus who suffered the torment of crucifixion. It was God himself. So, I should have told my friend that comparing himself to Jesus and trying to determine whose sufferings were worse is to misunderstand the whole point about the crucifixion. It is never about how much suffering Jesus was willing to take upon himself, and it is never about how much suffering we have to endure. It is about the fact that it was *God*, in Jesus, who suffered. I should therefore have asked my friend to look at the crucifixion and receive it as God's way of saying, "This is how much I love you, and this is how much I am involved in your life."

This is all very good, but how do such theological technicalities about God's love and involvement relate to our experience of spiritual loneliness? If I feel God is no longer with me, why would I believe Moltmann when he tells me that God loves me and is involved in my life? Why would his words have more authority than my experience that God is not at all present, but very absent? Moltmann would say to me, "God is involved." I would say back, "No, God is not involved." Word against word. We would have nothing more to discuss. Until, perhaps, I remember Jesus' cry on the cross, right before he slipped into death: "My God, my God, why have you forsaken me?"[11]

When I contemplate these words, Moltmann would say, I begin to understand that they make a difference. I see that Jesus' cry must be the loneliest cry ever uttered in the history of human existence. Not because it was brought on by the agony and the pain of a terrible death process. No, in ways I cannot understand, it was a cry of redemption where God himself experienced the absence of God. It was God experiencing spiritual loneliness, and crying out loud because God had left God alone. What greater spiritual loneliness can there possibly be? Right before my eyes, when Jesus cried out in loneliness on the cross, the world witnessed the most mysterious moment of redemption. It is how God unlocked the inner mechanics of the spiritual loneliness that haunts all of us. It was a moment within God, so to speak, where he both rejected himself and accepted his own rejection. When we understand this paradox, we understand Moltmann's mature theology.

I was thinking about this when I witnessed my dying friend struggle through a death process so agonizing I do not expect ever to witness anything like it again. Something about the situation made me suspect that God's redemption did not do for him what Moltmann tells me it is supposed to do. It looked to me like my suffering friend on one hand, and the suffering God on the other, were two entirely separate realities. They were like two ships passing each other in the dark night of an open sea. Both were monstrously real, but there was no communication between them. God's redemption did not reach into the deepest experience of my dying friend's spiritual loneliness and it did not heal the loneliness he experienced in relation to God. It did not bring him the comfort that God was with him in death.

The details of my friend's life during his last days are not entirely clear. He was moved to a different hospital and I could no longer visit him daily. I lost touch with him. Frankly, I think those who could be with him on a daily basis during his last days lost touch with him, too. The closer he came to death, the more he lived in a space where others could not follow him. As he slowly slipped away from us and started to exit this world, it also became increasingly evident that his faith was seriously challenged.

But, shortly after his funeral I had a dream. In this dream, it was a beautiful and sunny spring day. The windows of my second-floor apartment were wide open and I welcomed the scents of new life in the air. Suddenly I heard my friend call my name from outside. I recognized his voice and ran toward the door to meet him. He came running up the stairs in an old pair of jeans and a white t-shirt, just as I remembered him doing in real life. He was full of energy and, as he came up to me, he gave me a loving hug and said, "I just came to say goodbye."

The freedom and the joy he had in this dream stood in direct contrast to the way I remembered him from those long painful days on his deathbed. He resisted death so intensely while he was still alive that we could not say goodbye. It had been completely impossible. I believe my dream was rooted in the assurance that although his faith was challenged during that time, it was not lost. There is no doubt in my mind—not then, not now—that the resurrected Christ was there to meet him when he entered the next world.

I have doubts about something else, though. I doubt he experienced God's love and involvement during the time of his battle against death. I doubt he experienced God's love and I doubt he felt God's involvement in his suffering. As we watched him die, it was overwhelmingly painful to witness his fear. The loneliness that haunted him was so thick it was nearly tangible and there was an almost oppressive atmosphere of spiritual loneliness around him. He simply did not have confidence that God was with him and that God loved him. As a result, he could not let go of life. He died kicking and screaming, without the peace of faith. The way I will always think about his death is that he died in God's absence.

Much more seriously, I doubt my dying friend's spiritual loneliness *could* be healed by the understanding and the knowledge that God is a suffering God. He needed something more than that. But, of course! When we actually have to leave this world, cognitive understanding loses the comforting power it has when we are still alive and hopeful about our own future. No matter how well we understand God's redemptive work, we find ourselves spiritually lonely if all we have is cognitive knowledge of it. Knowledge cannot comfort someone who is consumed by the loneliness of God's absence.

I started this section by asking two questions. First, How does God help us in our suffering? Second, How do we receive that help? Christ's redemptive work answers the first. Contrary to our hope, however, it does not answer the second. That God died out of love for us does not automatically make us receptive to God's love. In what follows, I therefore want to pursue an answer to the second question. My goal is to find what Moltmann's theology of hope does not have, and to suggest why it did not have the power to comfort my dying friend in his death.

TRUE: CHRIST HEALS SPIRITUAL LONELINESS

Imagine yourself in love with a man who says he loves you, but who does not show his love to you. He is the man of your life, but he spends his time with others, gives physical affection to others, and is generous with others. All the while he somehow manages to withhold those same things from you. Although he keeps saying he loves you, you feel unwanted by him. Not knowing how else to deal with the situation, you decide to always speak highly of him and, no matter what, you keep smiling. As a result, other people do not notice that you walk through every day with his rejection constantly stabbing at your heart.

This is how Mother Teresa experienced her relationship with Jesus. She loved him but did not feel his love in return. She told other people about his love, watched them as they started to believe what she said about him and rejoiced when they reported that they had experienced his love for them. Yet, personally, she remained empty of his love. With her heart aching for him, she struggled to get through life on a daily basis and was not afraid of using graphic images to describe her situation. She compared herself to a newborn child left to die in a garbage can. Or she described herself as a person who was abandoned in the gutters to live like an animal. Just listen to what she says: "The physical situation of my poor left in the streets unwanted, unloved, unclaimed—are the true picture of my own spiritual life, of my love for Jesus."[12]

As well as any theologian or psychologist, Mother Teresa pointed right at the paradox that we can love God and give ourselves to him, but still remain spiritually lonely. She was lonely, not because she had no love for God, but because of her unreciprocated love and desire for him. "The more I want Him," she said, "the less I am wanted.—I want to love Him . . . and yet there is that separation—that terrible emptiness, that feeling of absence of God."[13] With painful irony, her situation was so much more severe because she persisted in her prayers that God's presence had to manifest in her heart in order for her to find consolation. She pleaded for God's love, but did not find it.

Instead, her prayers would return unanswered, as steel cold reminders of God's absence in her life. "When I try to raise my thoughts to Heaven—there is such convicting emptiness that those very thoughts return like sharp knives & hurt my very soul."[14] This emptiness and absence of God made her feel utterly lonely and deprived of his love: "I am told God loves me—and yet the reality of darkness & coldness & emptiness is so great that nothing touches my soul."[15] She asked her mentors and spiritual superiors to help her get through the darkness of this loneliness, but they could not help her. They were willing to help, but no one has the power to lift another person out of spiritual darkness.

Add to the intense pain of her situation that God never failed to provide for her sisters. They often testified that God answered prayers and gave them what they needed in their work. As one of them said: "Divine providence is always giving us in all ways unexpected. We just don't know where it is coming from. . . . It's such a delight to know that we don't really have to worry. No matter what we need and want for our people, it will be there. And even for ourselves, the way God provides for us is just fantastic."[16] Is it any wonder Mother Teresa thought of it as an experience of hell to live in such close proximity to God's love, to be an instrument of it, but to remain empty of God's love for herself? Listen to her words: "If there is hell—this must be one. How terrible it is to be without God—no prayer—no faith—no love."[17]

Of course, we should not forget that this spiritual loneliness was also a powerful positive drive in her, and it was easily the most significant reason for the success of her service to the poor. It gave her an enormous respect for the individual poor person because it was a practical way for her to identify with them. If poverty was anything for the poor to be ashamed of, it made her feel right at their level that she knew their shame firsthand. In her own loneliness, she knew she was as poor as they because she felt abandoned by God. Therefore, she had no need to look down at them. In fact, it set her free to speak correction, openly and directly, *up* to those who would speak down to them.

It is fascinating to watch her talk to authorities, or anyone else for that matter, and listen to her explaining to them that it is their best interest to learn from the poor. One instance of this happened when a well-meaning photographer approached her to take her picture for a grant application he wanted to submit on her behalf. In response to his request, she explained that her sisters were forbidden to do any fundraising, and then asked him to observe that rule too. Gently and gracefully, she refused him. What he really needed, she told him, was to know God's love for himself. With these instructions, she embraced his hand, gave him a blessing, and moved on with her day.[18]

Mother Teresa was no theologian and did not aspire to be one. She simply identified the needs of the poor, heard God ask her to address those needs, and then did what was necessary in order to complete the task. Hardly anyone fails to admire the selfless lifestyle she invested in this project. My instincts tell me, however, that her sacrificial lifestyle raises the bar too high for most of us. We admire her, but admit we could never do what she did. The sacrifices would be too much. No hot water? Possessing only two outfits, one on your body, and one in a plastic bag? Having practically no privacy, other than when you sleep, pray, or take time away from work to worship? So we end up watching her from a distance, much like we contemplate an icon of the ideal human being. It is handy to invoke her name when we need a moral boost and we refer to her as an example of what we call "a good person." But, she mostly makes us feel guilty and inadequate in our own limited service to others.

Because of her saintly status, I suspect those who revered Mother Teresa also had a difficult time accepting that she suffered a lifelong sense of rejection by God. Many reacted that way when it became public knowledge after her death. By the same token, however, I suspect many received the news with some relief. I certainly did. She had figured in my mind as a significant historical figure, but only peripherally because I could not identify with her. This changed when I started reading Father Brian Kolodiejchuk's book where he published some of her personal letters and reflected on her spiritual struggles.

I read it during a time in my own life that I can best describe metaphorically. It compares to the point in a marathon race where you have lost confidence that the race will ever end, and you forgot why you started running in the first place. Not that I am a marathon runner and really know what I am talking about, but I was so disconnected from God that I questioned my identity as a Christian. Life itself felt like a prison, because I did not understand why God kept withholding from me the basic things I needed in order to live a meaningful life on a daily basis. This made me spiritually lonelier than I care to admit. I was giving up on my belief that God was invested in my well-being. I did not doubt God's existence, or his goodness, only his willingness to provide for us according to his goodness.

It surprised me how explicit Mother Teresa was in her language and how directly she contributed her spiritual loneliness to God's will for her. Reading some of the most painful passages, it was difficult for me to understand why she did not just walk away from her relationship with Jesus and leave him alone. Why did she so willingly accept his rejection? Why did she believe God loved her when he did not make her feel his love for her? With all her smiles, was she not just uncritically passive and submissive? And why did she not conclude what many theologians already have, that if God acts this way, then he is not a God that we need to love and worship?

It would be entirely understandable, for instance, if she had agreed with Elie Wiesel who came to the personal conclusion about God that "I was not denying His existence, but I doubted His absolute justice."[19] I mean, how can she possibly say something as self-eradicating as this: "We must be living holocausts, for the world needs us as such"?[20] You would expect her to understand that if we wish to suffer the way the Jews suffered during World War II, then we are pretty much out of our minds.

Still, Mother Teresa's letters had a strange effect on me. Against my expectations, they convinced me that her acceptance of God's rejection was the primary drive behind the success of her work. I was surprised to find myself believing the most radical passages of her letters where she describes her simple choice to receive spiritual loneliness as God's will for her. These passages convinced me that the secret behind her work with the poor was willingness to embrace the suffering of feeling abandoned by God.

I realized that her choice to receive personal suffering as a privilege is what released her into a life of freedom that is unlike any other kind of freedom we can know. Spiritual loneliness remained a source of suffering for her but as she accepted it, it strangely also lost power over her. In a paradoxical way, she was free within her loneliness because she accepted it as God's will for her. I could no longer see her as an uncritical and submissive prisoner of God's will. Nor did she look like an untouchable icon of human goodness. Rather, she appeared as a fragile person who, because of her abandon to God's will for her, had no fear of anything this world could bring upon her. She was steeped in the sense that God, not she, was the author of her life and therefore nothing really had the power to touch her. No one could make demands on her and this was the secret freedom by which she opposed the destructive forces of poverty that continue to wreck our world.

I also began to see myself in Mother Teresa. Not because of her work with the poor, but because of the spiritual loneliness that haunted her no matter what she did to get rid of it. I realized that, although she primarily addressed physical poverty, the poverty of loneliness was a much deeper concern for her. "If you give a man a piece of bread," she said, "you have only satisfied one kind of hunger. Loneliness is a much more severe poverty."[21] There is no way around it. These words can only be the insight of someone who knows that no person is poorer than the lonely person, and that there is no disease worse than the loneliness of being unwanted and rejected. It was the understanding that she spoke out of a deeply personal experience of spiritual loneliness that finally caused me to pay attention to her story.

In particular, she made me rethink Jesus' experience of loneliness. As we know, Moltmann points to Jesus' cry on the cross as the most mysterious moment in the history of redemption. It was here, he says, that God suffered loneliness in relation to himself and somehow defeated the spiritual loneliness that haunts our world. But, Mother Teresa challenged Moltmann on this point and said that Jesus' loneliness was more severe in the garden of Gethsemane than it was on the cross. She noticed that he sweated blood in Gethsemane when he struggled to accept that he was about to suffer the impact of crucifixion. He did not actually do that during the crucifixion itself.[22] Of course, as my colleague, Dr. Amanda Quantz, wonders on this point: ". . . beaten, broken and crowned with thorns, who could tell one way or another whether Jesus sweat blood during the crucifixion?"[23] Although her point is well taken, I think it is safe to say that the writer of Luke's gospel wanted us to know how severely Jesus struggled to accept his call to die.

It could well be that the torture of loneliness in Gethsemane was worse for Jesus than the rejection and loneliness he experienced when he was actually dying. Both his friends and the Father were with him in the garden, but openly disengaged in his situation. His friends fell asleep and when he asked the Father to be spared from death, there was no response, only the appearance of an angel who offered him strength to persevere. The loneliness of this situation must have been nearly unbearable. In our own lives, many of us know the stabs of loneliness are hard to handle when we are alone, but often much harder when others are present and unresponsive to our need for consolation.

Reflecting on these things began to influence me in an unexpected way. I had subtle surges of joy come forward within me, of the kind I could not remember having since the time I first believed what the Christian scriptures say about Christ. I was captured by the backward idea that we tap into a source of freedom and empowerment when we have the courage to embrace our own spiritual loneliness. Going through some of the literature on the theology of suffering, I realized what I should have remembered from my New Testament studies, namely that the privilege of the Christian is to find joy in suffering. In concrete terms, I came across Pope John Paul II's encyclical, *Salvifici Doloris*, from 1984. It contained a simple formulation of the theological argument that all human suffering is participation in the sufferings of Christ. What helped me understand that this is a matter of joy was John Paul II's point that our suffering has direct value to God because he uses it to redeem the world. Today, right now and through the actual lives that we live.

So, how does John Paul II support this idea? First, he agrees that we can trust God to be involved in our lives because we have seen Christ willingly choose to suffer the full impact of crucifixion and death. This is, as we already know from Moltmann, the way God acted to redeem the world. But, John Paul II adds to this that redemption is also an invitation for us to understand our own suffering as part of Christ's suffering. For, as he says, "Christ has in a sense opened his own redemptive suffering to all human suffering."[24] Yes, Christ consoles us by coming into our suffering, as Moltmann would agree, but in addition to this, we also find consolation when we come into his. The thing is that we can bring our suffering into him, and then it is no longer really our suffering, but his. When we do this, we somehow complete this double reality of suffering: we receive Christ into our suffering and we hand our suffering over to him so it can be to his free use.

It is in the mystery of this double reality of suffering that we are privileged to discover the purpose of our suffering, even when it does not make sense. Plus, we accept our sufferings as the sufferings of Christ, and our loneliness as the loneliness of Christ, and then realize the whole thing is much less cognitive than practical. As John Paul II says, "Christ does not explain in the abstract the reason for suffering, but before all else he says: 'Follow me!' Come! Take part through your suffering in this work of saving the world, a salvation achieved through my suffering! Through my Cross."[25] There is nothing magical about this call to follow, mostly because it does not make our sufferings go away. Rather, it is something we can only experience as a process that requires the investment of time.

Likewise, the joy that comes to us through the process of embracing our suffering is something that takes time to receive, too. "Gradually, *as the individual takes up his cross*, spiritually uniting himself to the Cross of Christ, the salvific meaning of suffering is revealed before him. . . . It is then that man finds in his suffering interior peace and even spiritual joy."[26] I believe it was this kind of joy I began to experience when I realized that my spiritual loneliness could be significant to God. It did not make my loneliness go away, but it gave me hope that God was somehow putting it to use for his purpose of redeeming the world. The insight that God is still in the process of redeeming the world, and that he uses human suffering to that end, became an invitation for me to experience my own loneliness as an investment in that process. It added new meaning to St. Paul's statement, "I am now rejoicing in my sufferings."[27]

Let us be clear and let us not fool ourselves. There is no joy in the actual embracing of our suffering. It hurts, and that is all there is to say about it, which is why our natural inclination is to protest against suffering as long as we can. When, however, we do find the courage and begin to accept our suffering as it comes to us, then we are, slowly and simultaneously, *"overcoming ... the sense of the uselessness of suffering."*[29] Plus, we get a glimpse of divine love as something entirely different from what we like to think of as love. We realize God's love does not come as the pleasant flutter of the heart that most of us like to associate with love. Rather, it creates in us a willingness to believe, against our will, and against our best judgment about God's intensions for us. It feels as if faith takes over and starts telling us that no suffering proves to us that God's promises cannot be trusted.

This, I believe, is the reason Mother Teresa could not turn her back on Jesus and did not leave him alone when she felt most lonely and rejected by him. Even if she wanted to leave him, she was like a captive of her own faith. In the midst of her suffering, the power of faith kept her from leaving Jesus. She may not have experienced God's love tangibly, and she may have lacked tangible joy in her faith, but she was never overcome by the sense that suffering is useless. She did not doubt that God knew what he was doing with her, or that she could trust him. Hence, a journalist asked her, "Were you not for a second in doubt? After all, Christ himself had moments of doubt. In Gethsemane." And her response was this:

> No. There was no doubt. . . . The moment you accept, the moment you surrender yourself, that's the conviction. But it may mean death to you, eh? The conviction comes the moment you surrender yourself. Then there is no doubt. The moment Jesus said, "Father, I am at your disposal, Thy will be done," He had accepted. That was His agony. . . . Once you have got God within you, that's for life. There is no doubt.[30]

Perhaps Mother Teresa did not experience much joy in her suffering because her spiritual loneliness was so oppressive. But, this lack of joy did not cause her to abandon the promise that her sufferings were important for God's purposes.

What I miss in Moltmann, and what my dying friend desperately needed in his struggle against death, was personal assurance that suffering is meaningful. For Moltmann, the suffering of spiritual loneliness does not have such meaning but is something from which God must redeem us. For Mother Teresa, the absence of suffering could never be the goal of redemption, because suffering itself *is* redemption.

THREE

Social Loneliness and the Fellowship of the Holy Spirit

THE FIRST TIME I experienced social loneliness, and was aware of it, happened on the evening I went to my first real school party. The event was very important because I was now old enough to attend these parties. I had been taking professional sewing lessons for a while, and it had already resulted in some nice clothes. I am telling you this so you understand how excited I was about this party. I knew some of my peers would prepare for it by drinking alcohol, but in my mind that faded in comparison to the kick I would get from wearing this particular pair of funky white pants I had just made.

It was when I entered the school building with my best friend, and walked toward the party hall, that loneliness suddenly descended upon me with the weight of a monster beanbag. For the first time in my life I experienced social loneliness and I knew it. I was with other people but I still felt lonely. Probably I had been socially lonely before, but never with such intense awareness of it. There were a good hundred people present, and I knew most of them. I knew their siblings, their parents, and the houses where they lived. Our town was a place of childhood comfort for most of us, so we generally knew each other. But the loneliness? That was a new acquaintance. I knew I belonged with these people but I suddenly felt like a stranger in their company.

Looking back, I think of this event as the kind of experience most of us have when we are coming of age and realize the world is so much bigger than we first thought. It is a natural part of our maturation process and we learn to handle these temporary loneliness spells, just as we learn to handle so many other unpleasant things in life. At the same time, I also think of this event as a first inkling of the deep and unsettling sense of social loneliness we can experience as human beings.

Now fast forward about two decades. At that point I had lived a couple of years as a foreigner in America, which was long enough for the initial sense of excitement about "life abroad" to subside. I was familiar with American culture, enjoyed daily life with people I liked, had made friends I knew would be for life, and belonged to a supportive faith community. And then something occurred that made me conscious of social loneliness in a way I had never been before, including back at that school party.

I was invited to dinner by a Danish American family. Earlier that week, the husband had expressed how thrilled he was to meet me because, as he said, "It is so rare and nice to meet a fellow Dane." I shared his sentiment and was excited when he and his wife invited me to their house. I was looking forward to the evening, and we had a wonderful time of sharing stories and backgrounds. Our connection was immediate. After dinner, the children took off and my hosts brought out an atlas because they wanted to see where I grew up. We were sitting next to each other on the couch and the husband leafed eagerly through the pages of, first, The Middle East, then Eastern Europe, Italy and Southern Europe, Germany, Scandinavia, Denmark, England, and Ireland. Not finding what he was looking for, he started leafing backward again, frustrated that he could not find the map of Denmark.

I am not sure why I had been quiet when we were both looking at Denmark on the map and he kept leafing past it. Perhaps I was beginning to wonder about the larger implications of a situation where I was sitting next to a Danish person who did not know what Denmark looks like. This was especially noteworthy to me since any five-year old Dane knows how strikingly the Danish coasts follow the contours of an old hunch-backed person with a large dripping nose, leaning slightly forward, and wearing a slanted hood. In any case, I left the dinner thinking this evening might foreshadow something important about my future life in America. I contemplated the prospect of a lifestyle where I would always be a foreigner, even in the company of those who shared my background. It could well be that life in America would involve an ever deepening sense of social loneliness.

Around this same time someone sent me a Danish magazine featuring an interview with the Scandinavian film and television director, Bille August. The interviewing journalist was particularly interested to know why Bille had decided against making what looked like a clever career move to America after his success with film projects like *Pelle the Conquerer, The House of the Spirits*, and *The Adventures of Young Indiana Jones*. His answer was simple and stuck to my mind like glue. He said, "I do not want to live the life of an immigrant." Sniffing up the stinging smells of not belonging, he had decided to stay in Scandinavia where he belonged. Now I was asking myself if I should perhaps follow his lead. Did I want to embrace a future where I risked losing my deepest sense of belonging? What if I would begin to feel so much at home in America that I would become a foreigner back in Denmark? Could I handle the social loneliness of that?

In my own mind, I argued that social loneliness is so much part of the fabric of American culture that it connects people in a community all of its own. After all, most Americans claim to be "from somewhere else," which is partly why America is a place where immigrants generally feel comfortable. If you lack a sense of belonging, you can feel at home in this country because most other people lack the same sense of belonging. That is what I kept rehearsing for myself.

At the same time, I knew America was still the land of opportunities and it was beginning to grow on me. Quite literally it felt like I was developing what Philip Slater decades ago called the "traveler's antennae." He described these antennae as a person's "sensitivity to nuances of custom and attitude that helps her adapt and make her way in strange settings."[1] I have always thrived on experiences that feed this sensitivity because nothing makes you feel more alive, free, and creative. Living more permanently in America, I was beginning to count on the foreigner's quiet but steady sense of being alive to new things. People and situations were never entirely predictable to me, and this added excitement to my daily life. Ironically, therefore, the discomfort of my deepening sense of social loneliness gave me the added bonus of a fulfilling lifestyle on a daily basis. So, although I did not decide to stay in America, I never got around to leaving.

What does all this have to do with the fellowship of the Holy Spirit? Before answering that question, I want to address this next question. If social loneliness is indeed an important part of the fabric of American culture, is it fair to say that Americans are particularly lonely? Yes, social scientists say. It may not look like it, but we are warned not to be deceived. Laura Pappano, for instance, argues that although we are not lonely in the old traditional sense of the word, we are "the overstimulated, hyperkinetic, overcommitted, striving, under-cared-for, therapy dependent, plugged in, logged on, sleep deprived. *We are the new lonely.*[2] She says we exhaust ourselves into a serious relational disconnect from others.

Pappano thinks our marketdriven culture has spilled over into our relationships. We fear misusing other people's goodwill toward us, and we feel obliged to pay our friends back when they do us a favor. Quietly, we therefore agree to play a social game where "marketers and purveyors of material culture are trying to sell what we crave: social connection."[3] Personal relationships have more or less become commercial interactions. We negotiate with each other. The social signals we send sound something like this: "If you will be my friend, then I will be yours." The problem is, underneath these superficial connections, we are very lonely.

The General Social Survey (GSS) has empirical evidence to support Pappano's instincts. In a period of approximately two decades (1985–2004), the statistics are as follows. "The number of people saying there is no one with whom they discuss important matters nearly tripled."[4] In an article from *The Washington Post*, Smith-Lovin comments on this GSS survey that, "Compared with 1985, nearly 50 percent more people in 2004 reported that their spouse is the only person they can confide in."[5] This means Americans have rapidly shrinking social networks and significantly fewer personal confidants than only two decades ago. Of course, a spouse can be a confidant and does give us a sense of companionship, but he or she can never be our social network.[6]

With these loneliness numbers in mind, it is hard not to think of Robert Putnam's book, *Bowling Alone*. Both in regard to the social crisis it describes and the solution it suggests. Putnam gives us statistics that show we are no longer as active in social groups as we used to be. We are quite simply no longer as eager to become members of groups like political parties, professional organizations, and churches. There was an increase in that kind of group membership right after World War II and the numbers kept rising until the late 1950s when they reached a plateau. But then they dropped dramatically from the early 1960s all the way up until the late 1990s.[7]

Putnam thinks this development is unfortunate but not hopeless. America has been a culture of loneliness before and recovered from it.[8] Right now, he says, we could well be at the lowest point of a curve that is about to go back up. So, we should have "the optimistic hope that social reformers might invent new forms of social capital to replace the dying forms."[9] What would drive such a social reform is not clear, but Putnam mentions electronic communication. In the early 2000s, he did not know social media were the next social phenomena on the horizon, and it is interesting to imagine that the Internet would be a solution to our social loneliness. Especially because we love to think of online communication as an enemy of personal relationships.[10] Whether or not this will happen, Putnam expects our culture will keep oscillating between making us socially lonely and helping us be socially connected.

Now, think about the Holy Spirit coming into this world in which we go back and forth between being very lonely and being not so lonely. As Putnam emphasizes, it is challenging enough to navigate the social world of human interaction; adding the spiritual presence of God into these social fluctuations puts one more player in the game and makes our situation even more challenging. Suddenly we draw on two different resources when we connect with other people: our social skills and the Holy Spirit. On the one hand, we are naturally social beings and do not need divine assistance in order to connect with each other and become less lonely. On the other hand, God creates a unique kind of social connection between people when the Holy Spirit comes into the world. These are two different ways for social connections to develop and it can be both confusing and frustrating to navigate both of them simultaneously.

Here is an example of what I mean. We come to church and expect to find a unique social fellowship because we know the Holy Spirit lives in everyone there and we know the church is under God's guidance. And, that is what we find. Many people testify that had it not been for their church community, their lives would be in shambles. The community of the Holy Spirit has this kind of transforming and healing power. Usually, however, we come to a point where we have to acknowledge that social life within the church develops much like social life outside the church. Those who have the Holy Spirit develop social conflicts as much as anyone else. In fact, conflicts within the church can be more painful than conflicts outside the church because we often develop high expectations of each other as God's people. We think that, of all people, Christians should know how to love and respect one other, and when we fall short of that ideal, the disappointment can be severe.

What concerns me most about this kind of disappointment is that feelings of loneliness often follow right on the heels of it. In fact, it is not uncommon to meet people in the church who feel lonelier there than they do in secular social contexts. It is unfortunate but revealing to hear Christians describe their faith community along the lines of what this fifty year old engineer concluded about his: "The Church is cold and lacking in any kind of brotherliness. Two Scouts, two men from the same school or the same Army unit are more brotherly than two Catholics."[11] The expectations he brought into the church and what he actually found there did not match. We can only imagine how he must have left church with a heart that was unfulfilled in its longing for meaningful relationships.

But, what if we could educate our expectations? What if we could learn to be more aware of the fact that while we are united in the Holy Spirit, we are also just regular human beings with natural social skills that sometimes work well, but sometimes do not? Perhaps immigrants are particularly sensitive to this possibility and perhaps it takes something like an intimate experience with the lifestyle of a foreigner to gain the insight we find in Joseph Soloveitchik. "Comfort in one's religious family is no guarantee of comfort and meaning within the larger community."[12] His distinction is clear. It is one thing for us to be socially connected because the Holy Spirit lives in us. But it is another to develop social connections with each other because that is what we naturally do as human beings.

I want to talk about the process where I realized my own hopes for the fellowship of the Holy Spirit were too high. I do that in the next section where I also develop the argument that the fellowship of the Holy Spirit does not heal our social loneliness. I follow that argument with a section where I say the opposite, namely that the Hoy Spirit within us indeed does create a social community where loneliness no longer haunts us. As you read along, consider these opposing argument an invitation for you to reflect on both possibilities and to decide for yourself what you think.

NOT TRUE: THE FELLOWSHIP OF THE HOLY SPIRIT HEALS SOCIAL LONELINESS

It was when I first developed a sense of social loneliness as a foreigner in America, that I also became part of a spiritually attractive church community I will call The Church. I had never before experienced the fellowship of the Holy Spirit as strongly as I did there. I could not help thinking that Yves Congar accurately describes our fellowship when he says that God's church is "the mystical communion of which the Holy Spirit is the sovereign principle."[13] Together, we prayed for big things and small things and learned both to wait for God's answer and to receive his provisions when they came. Sometimes God answered in quiet ways, sometimes in more spectacular ways. Either way, it was in this atmosphere of anticipation that I started thinking this fellowship of the Holy Spirit would help me overcome my social loneliness in America.

My years at The Church were also transformative at a personal level, and I was privileged to be part of the community until I accepted a new teaching position and had to relocate. I know my years there taught me things about the spiritual life that will benefit me for the rest of my life. How can I exaggerate the significance of learning to cooperate with God as he sets us free from psychological, spiritual, or physical pains we have endured most of our lives? And how can I exaggerate the significance of discovering that freedom in Christ is more personally satisfying than any other freedom we can have?

Hardly anything inspires the life of faith more than to realize how willingly God gives us good things. Personally, it gave me a new frame of thinking about my own faith, and I often think of it as a parallel to Peter's situation when he acted on Jesus' invitation to step out of his boat and found himself walking on water. It must have been challenging for him to process the experience afterward and maybe he wondered if it had happened at all. If his faith was fragile in the situation, it was probably no stronger later, when he evaluated it. It must have been a surreal experience for him and he must have felt both empowered and powerless at the same time. I mean, how can you categorize an event that is entirely God's doing, but at the same time would not have happened without your desire to participate? If there is a spiritual equivalent to the taste of a sweet-and-sour sauce, this must be it.

As a theologian, I think of an experience like this as a practical version of Karl Barth's idea of revelation. Not the Book of Revelation, but revelation as it happens every time God chooses to speak to us. Barth thinks of revelation as God showing us something we could not otherwise know. Just as St. Paul, who says that "what can be known about God is plain . . . because God has shown it."[14] Barth also thinks all God's revelations are designed to give us a deeper understanding of Jesus Christ, because somehow they always point to him. The more complex insight, however, and what helped me understand my experience at The Church, is Barth's

THE POWER OF ONE

point that every time God speaks to us, it is as if we hear him simultaneously pronounce these two words to us: "Yes" and "No."

Yes, God sent Jesus into the world to live and die for us, which we must take as a positive affirmation of who we are. But, No, God has no confidence in us, which is exactly what he is trying to communicate by sending Jesus into our world. Yes, God is personally committed to us with all that he is. But, No, we deserve judgment, and we are hopelessly lost if we are left on our own. In a word, Barth tells us that to encounter Jesus is to face God's love and God's judgment in one and the same event.

Thinking about my experience at The Church in this light, I first thought God spoke more Yes than No over us. When things later became difficult, and our fellowship began to crack, I started thinking it was the other way around and that God spoke more No than Yes over us. In the end, however, I needed to accept that God's Yes and No had both been true for us all along. As a community, we should probably have paid more attention to this teaching. We should have been quicker to remember that when we hear God speak a comforting Yes to us through Jesus, somewhere in the tone of his voice is always a No. There is no way for us to have one without the other. I just did not see it, could not see it, or refused to see it. Either way, I should have seen it, and let me explain why.

When I first started attending The Church, it felt to me as if something was not quite right about the social glue that held us together. There was an atmosphere of social loneliness, except it was hard to detect because we spoke very highly and respectfully of one another. My first impression was that people loved and respected one another more generously here than in most church communities I had known. Over time, however, it appeared to me that much of the social life of The Church was held up by a silent expectation that we would acknowledge each other's assets and lovingly let the rest go unmentioned. It is a wonderful thing for a community to have and to observe house rules of loving and respectful interaction. That was not the problem. The problem was a sense of denial about the social disconnect that ran as an unpleasant current underneath all that love.

Maybe I would have paid closer attention to this undercurrent if I had already been more attentive to Dietrich Bonhoeffer's writing on ecclesiology and theological anthropology. (These are technical terms and what he means by them will become clear as we move on.) Unfortunately, that is not what I did, so I have been reading Bonhoeffer again, looking for some retrospective understanding. Let me share my thoughts.

The ministry of prayer was a particularly vibrant part of the daily life and routines at The Church. We learned how to pray for one another and if I had a personal need, there was always someone I could ask to pray for me. He or she would do it as naturally as giving directions to the nearest post office. It was easy and comfortable because the person would know how to be concerned for me but also how to present that concern to God and leave it there. We learned we had to avoid thinking we were in a position to solve other people's problems, because that would make our prayers and concerns manipulative. In this way, our community was one of loving care for the well-being of others. It fostered an overall atmosphere of deep appreciation for one another, for the visitor, and for the stranger, and it created a strong sense of spiritual unity.

I liked this, and I think Bonhoeffer would have liked it too. Mostly because it illustrates one of the two ideas that constitute the heartbeat of his theological anthropology. The idea is the following. You are the person God created you to be when you encounter other people and find yourself ethically responsible for their well-being and simply love the fact that they exist. If we look a little closer at this idea, then we discover why it is important for Bonhoeffer to think of love and ethical responsibility as inseparable. It also helps us understand why his anthropology must be theological in nature and why he defines the human being as a creature who cannot possibly *not* relate to God.

You constantly have opportunities to be the person God created you to be. You encounter someone and experience the familiar tug inside where both of you know you are free to go, but you also know you are bound to stay. It is as simple as the feeling you get when you see someone who needs help, and you are inclined to give a hand. You know what I am talking about because it is that naturally respectful love we all experience on a regular basis. Bonhoeffer wants us to pay attention to this inclination to help others because it gives our life a quality it could not possibly have otherwise. It puts us in our right element because we suddenly know what it means to be a human person. It is the encounter with other people that sets us up to be at our very best: fully human.

Bonhoeffer thinks the best example we have of this is from the creation of Adam and Eve when they first met. Adam was asleep and had no idea what was happening. But, waking up, "Adam knows that God has made use of the human, has taken a piece of the sleeping human body, and has formed the other person from it. And it is with a true cry of joy that Adam recognizes the woman [Weib]: 'This at last is bone of my bones and flesh of my flesh. She shall be called woman [Männin] because she was taken out of man.'"[15] Adam came alive to a realization of himself because someone else was there, next to him, living and breathing, and of his own kind.

The important point about the example of Adam and Eve is what Bonhoeffer says next: "Eve, the other person, was the limit given to Adam in bodily form. He acknowledged this limit in love . . . he loved it precisely in its nature as a limit for him."[16] In order to understand this comment, we should remember that Adam had already spent a long time naming all the animals. As God had watched Adam interact with all the animals that were different form him, he decided to create a second one of Adam's kind. The reason the two human beings were then able to find love together was the fact that they were a match of equals. They were the same, and were therefore individuals who naturally challenged each other merely by being present in each other's lives. This means that the moment they recognized each other as equals, they also knew God intended for them to serve one another. Each of them was the reason the other one encountered his or her own limitation. Or, to put it a little differently, human love and human being became possible when Adam and Eve could not just do whatever they wanted because there was someone else there who required recognition.

If we were to take Bonhoeffer's idea all the way, I venture to say that Adam could not have been truly human before the creation of Eve. Perhaps it was not even until the creation of Eve that God had in fact created the first human being. Only with her could they know themselves and their own limits, because then the other one was there to remind them of those limits. Also, it was only with the creation of Eve that they had a full experience of themselves as God's creatures. Not until they realized that God intentionally gave them to each other could they know he was involved in their existence.

Ever since then, love is what we all do and what we all desire. Like Adam, all of us are restless because we need to know our own limit, and it is always another person who is the solution to this need. When you enter my space, you become that limit to me, which is something I desperately need in order to be comfortable with myself and to know who I am. And you need me to do the same for you. This is what Bonhoeffer means when he says that being human is to live a life where love and ethical responsibility are inseparable. We can only love others if we first respect them in such a way that we desire their well-being. If we understand this about the nature of being human, then we understand the first important idea of Bonhoeffer's theological anthropology.

Now, let me take this idea back to The Church. Many of the people I met there, and developed relationships and friendships with over time, were independent individuals. Independent in the sense of being secure in themselves and knowing that setting and maintaining healthy relational boundaries is a good thing. Good for oneself and good for others, because it set us free to seek guidance from the Holy Spirit before we responded to each other's needs. Much in the way Bonhoeffer talks about Adam and Eve being limits to one another. I already spoke of this independence in connection with our ministry of prayer, but now wonder if our independence might not have contributed to the social loneliness that haunted us. It is my hunch that it did, because it often seemed that the most important thing about us was our personal boundaries. This made it difficult to connect at a deeper and meaningful level. Not impossible, just difficult.

I think we feared what we could lose if we made ourselves vulnerable to others before we thought it was safe. I also think this fear was driven by a subtle but powerful pull that compelled many of us to develop a certain pattern of interaction with God and others. Most of us had experienced God in extraordinary ways, and continued to come back for more of the same. The good fruit of this was a growing trust in God's faithfulness. But, somewhere along the line, many of us had also become fearful that we might miss out on the magic of it all. We somehow thought this could happen if we jeopardized our connection to those who had successfully helped us receive from God in the past.

The invisible structure of authority that evolved around this situation was unhealthy and it influenced the way we related to each other. We were careful not to disclose what could potentially put us out of favor with those we had silently agreed were in charge. We hoped for their affirmation and acceptance and behaved in ways we thought would give us access to those things. In turn, they were just as cautious about self-disclosure as everyone else. So, by all of us holding our watchful distance, we gently kept each other in check. In reality, in this local fellowship of the

Holy Spirit, we created something like a celebrity culture, and it was not always the Holy Spirit who was the lead star.

Thinking about this celebrity factor reminds me of an interview Bob Dylan gave on 60 Minutes in 2004. He told of an incident where a fan came to his door to discuss organic farming, of which Dylan knew "not a thing," as he said. This fan's confidence in Dylan was clearly out of proportion, as we all know is the case with the confidence we place in celebrities. We think because a person has authority in one area, he or she naturally has authority in other areas too. The flip-side of this situation is of course that no celebrity is immune to the flattery of an admiring crowd. Dylan's entire lifestyle, for instance, is one of feeding on excessive admiration. It is not for no reason he is on a "never ending tour" and practically lives on the road.

Things were not nearly that extreme at The Church, but they were not entirely different either. As a result, we generated what I think of as a culture of controlled vulnerability. Many of us struggled with an unsettling kind of loneliness because we were carefully watching each other and ourselves. This watchfulness was hard to detect in oneself, and I experienced it as almost impossible to shake off. I think it was often tied to a secret desire either to be or not to be associated with certain people. This, of course, had to evolve into an experience of disillusionment. It was hard to accept that even this fellowship, where the presence and the guidance of the Holy Spirit was so strong, left us struggling with a sense of being lonely among others.

Someone like Martin Buber would probably be right on this situation as a perfect case study for one of his most famous theological concerns. As early as 1922, he is bemoaning the fact that people's ability to form relationships are fast disintegrating. He calls the phenomenon "a progressive increase of the It-world,"[17] which is to say that he thinks people relate to each other as objects more than real persons. This, he argues, is the same as selfishly isolating and detaching oneself. Unfortunately, this makes the difference between an ego and a person. Here is how he describes that difference: "Egos appear by setting themselves apart from other egos. Persons appear by entering into relation to other persons."[18] Buber considers it a sad reality that, whereas persons develop intimate relationships by "touching" others, egos use others to distinguish themselves. "I am this, and definitely not that," an ego says, and creates a distance to others. Most of us behave like egos and still try to develop community, not realizing this is basically an impossible project.

Buber thinks people could solve this problem by encountering each other the way an I encounters a You: as vulnerable, authentic beings and with an attitude of mutual exchange. Interestingly, Bonhoeffer says exactly the same thing, only a generation later. So, both Buber and Bonhoeffer argue that we need a theological anthropology to help us get a sense of how to be more fully human. Except, they envision this happening in very different ways. It is Buber's vision that we should break down the barriers that separate us and develop more intimate relationship with each other. In contrast, Bonhoeffer wants us to use those barriers positively and think of them as boundaries that help us define who we are as individuals. He thinks being aware of these boundaries would give us a better sense of who we are in separation from others. It would also give us a better chance at serving each other and connecting more authentically.[19]

Which one of these two solutions could we have used at The Church? If we had followed Buber's lead and become more intimate with each other, could we have done a better job steering clear of social loneliness? Or did we need Bonhoeffer to help us get a better understanding of our personal limitations and learn how to better serve one another and live more authentically? In other words, did we need help from Buber or from Bonhoeffer?

Let me suggest that we find an answer to this question if we turn to the second important idea in Bonhoeffer's theological anthropology. We already understand the significance of his first idea (that love and ethical responsibility are inseparable, and that we only become fully human if we both serve and love others). Now I want to pay some attention to his second idea, which will help me show why I think following Buber's advice to become more intimate would not have been enough to get rid of our social loneliness. First, though, I need to share my impressions of some social patterns that characterized life at The Church over a period of some years. Then I want to indicate how Bonhoeffer, not Buber, could have helped us with our problem of social loneliness.

First, The Church went through a season of excitement and a strong sense of unity around the vision of becoming the community God desired it to be. This developed into a fruitful season of growth, both for us as individuals and for the community at large. Unfortunately, this growth somehow intensified and developed into a season of conflicts. These conflicts became deeper because some groups found it difficult to pursue their vision for the community. With almost organic predictability, these groups would develop a conviction that they needed to leave the community, which they did. Things would then settle down and a new sense of excitement about the future started to rebuild among those who did not leave. This meant a positive return to a vision for the community's future. Except, the cycle repeated itself and conflicts developed all over again.

Anyone familiar with the pain and disillusionment involved in a marriage divorce also knows how painful it is to go through a church divorce. When a vital part of a fellowship feels the need to distance itself, and eventually leaves, it is rarely a pretty process. Well into it, the social entanglements it creates often make it nearly impossible for anyone to give an accurate account of what is going on. Unfortunately, it is rarely of much help that everyone strives to speak truthfully and be both wise and mature. Most are still hurt and get caught in feelings of confusion and disillusionment.

What struck me as the most puzzling aspect of our church divorces was the apparent ease with which close friendships were terminated. I already described the spiritual unity it gave to communicate with one another and God in an atmosphere of spiritual fellowship. Now I realized the negative influence our spiritual bonds could also have on our friendships. In some instances, the spiritual aspects of our relationships became more significant than the personal aspects. Some of us started thinking that, for the sake of spiritual self-protection, it was necessary to end personal friendships. Sadly, the power of strong relationships first helped build a sense of unity, and later contributed with equal power to the disintegration of that unity.

Conflicts we could have solved within the context of personal relationships were loaded with more spiritual significance than they could carry. It was a sad consequence of this that we ended up divorcing people we both loved and respected. Not unlike Adam and Eve when they distanced themselves from each other because they lost sight of their discovery that they needed each other in order to be fully human. I think the atmosphere of controlled vulnerability we had generated as part of our celebrity culture made it easier for us to withdraw from friends. Because we were already withholding ourselves from each other, it was easier to terminate relationships. Not easy, just easier.

During our church divorces, many of us were like wounded animals, trying to rescue ourselves from broken friendships and broken hopes. The pain we were willing to bring upon ourselves was heartbreaking, and it makes me return to one of Barth's more striking comments. Here is what he says: "Tears are closer to us than laughter. We stand more deeply in No than in Yes."[20] Prior to this comment, Barth had just tried to convince us that God speaks a simultaneous Yes and No over us. Now he corrects that and says that the No describes us more accurately than the Yes. It is interesting that Bonhoeffer agrees with Barth on this point. In fact, it is exactly the same thing Bonhoeffer argues in the second idea of his theological anthropology. Namely that our most fundamental problem as human beings is our tendency to destroy each other's experience of social belonging. What Barth calls a No, Bonhoeffer thinks of as social loneliness.

How does God's No to us describe social loneliness in a Christian fellowship? We can begin answering this by looking at Bonhoeffer's claim that one of our biggest problems is a tendency to idealize St. Paul's idea that we are the body of Christ.[21] For some reason, we think this means we are endowed with a unique capacity for purity and holiness. But, Bonhoeffer wants us to understand that we, as the body of Christ, are not particularly holy on the whole. It is more accurate to say that we live in "the hard contradiction between the actuality and the reality of human holiness."[22] Or that we constantly experience a tension between those parts of us that are holy, and those that are not.

Yes, we are holy because we live in Christ and he lives in us. But, No, we cannot point to any Christian fellowship and say, "There he is! There is the body of Christ, the holy one!" Holiness is as invisible as the kingdom that "is not coming with things that can be observed,"[23] as Jesus said. Saying this, Jesus practically refuted the idea that we can claim to *be* the kingdom because the kingdom of God is among us, but in such a way that we cannot easily detect it. When we start to deny this, we commit the sin of thinking much too highly of ourselves.

I agree with Clifford Green's reading of Bonhoeffer because he leaves no doubt that the greatest enemy of Christian community is the sin of Christians. We all have a tendency to deny that we need others in order to be fully human, which is the same as deliberately refusing to be what we are created to be, namely human. Bonhoeffer thinks of this as a deliberate act where we place ourselves in "a state of radical separation from God and other human beings."[24] This makes us lonely, but even more seriously, we also make *others* lonely that way. It therefore makes a lot of sense when Bonhoeffer says our sin can cause our church community to degenerate into "an institution for the systematic exploitation of one by the other."[25] It is a sad thing that we exploit the fellowship where we belong, but this is what we do when we think we can live without others.

Whether or not you agree that Bonhoeffer's theology is essentially about social dynamics like these, it is hard not to be struck by his understanding that "sin is the exercise of a self-serving *power* over others."[26] Or that sin encourages "centrality of power, dominance, and exploitation."[27] When I read passages like these, I can see how there must be an almost organic interaction between sociality as a positive drive, and sin as a negative drive. When we are fully human, as we are created to be, then we inevitably form good Christian community and relate to each other in love and respect. But when we commit the sin of isolating ourselves from others, then we cause Christian community to disintegrate.

I believe these positive and negative drives determined the social patterns at The Church. We were haunted by the one enemy that is most dangerous to any community. It was the sin of individuals thinking they could be themselves in separation from others. This sin sent our community through cycles of building spiritual and social unity, breaking that unity, and then recreating it. We were building social unity because we were humans and that is what humans do best. But we were also contributing to the disintegration of that same social unity because we were committing the sin of isolating ourselves individually.

I need to add a technical comment about Bonhoeffer's ecclesiology here. The term ecclesiology refers to the way the New Testament authors thought about the Christian church (from the Greek, *ecclesia*), or the community of those who followed Christ. The interesting thing about Bonhoeffer's understanding of ecclesiology is that he considers it synonymous with theological anthropology. His reasoning for this is simple because the moment we understand what it means to be human, we automatically also understand what it means to be a community. There is no way for us to be fully human without creating community. Because to be human is to be together. Even though being a human and being a community are two different things, they are still two sides of the same coin.

Let me now close this section with the conclusion that the Holy Spirit does not heal social loneliness. Even though such healing is what

God desires, and it is why he sends the Holy Spirit to unite us, the sins of Christians cause our communities to disintegrate. We hope for communal belonging, and we trust God can give it to us. But, regardless of how much spiritual comfort we can find in the fellowship of the Holy Spirit, it is never enough to heal social loneliness. But then again, we should not be surprised by this, because it is still by hope that we believe God's people will give us an experience of complete belonging. A hope that is still to be consummated.

TRUE: THE FELLOWSHIP OF THE HOLY SPIRIT HEALS SOCIAL LONELINESS

One of the more paradoxical experiences I have had is my conversion. It was mostly a matter of spiritual manipulation and happened in relation to a youth camp leader who was convinced that God wants us to have a certain kind of spiritual experience. His vision was that all followers of God should be baptized in the Holy Spirit. When he met me, he therefore navigated me into a situation where he could pray for me, and even though nothing happened, he then pressured me to give public testimony to the contrary. I was young, did not know what else to do, and gave him what he wanted.

I was already a theology student at the university when this happened but had yet to read Karl Barth. This was unfortunate because I later realized that his theology could have helped me counter the spiritual manipulation I experienced at the youth camp. So, we should take a closer look at his theology. The thing about Barth is that he was passionately opposed to any and all types of Christianity that make claims to even vague predictions of what God will do or say. You may argue that he was criticizing organized Christianity, but that is not entirely accurate. He was a more sophisticated thinker than that and wanted to bring every individual person's faith under a theological microscope, not just organized Christianity.

We can know what God did in the past, Barth said, but God is under no obligation to act in the future in ways he acted in the past. This is how independent God is from us, and to forget that is to place constrictions on God. We should refrain from this and allow God to be transcendent and beyond our comprehension. In an effort to make this point clear, Barth famously said that "God may speak to us through Russian communism or a flute concerto, a blossoming shrub or a dead dog."[28] A dead dog! That is the kind of power and transcendent freedom we are dealing with in the God of Christians. This God is free to do what he wants and we cannot change that.

Barth used such radical imagery because he believed it conveyed the truth, but also because he was up against the rising powers of German Nazism. He needed to match the strength of the Nazis and this shaped his theology. The Nazi party was bringing unreasonable suffering upon the European countries and he needed to speak of a transcendent God who was strong enough to counter this evil force. Also, Barth spoke up against Adolf Hitler's utopian promises and wanted to show how danger-ous he thought they were. Part of his opposition against Hitler was to refuse pledging allegiance to him. In 1935, this cost him suspension as a teacher in Germany, and it forced him to move back to Switzerland where he was born.

Interestingly, personal sympathy with the Jews did not concern Barth much. It provoked him much more that the German Christians had al-lowed the Nazi party to manipulate them in the first place. Christian lead-ers should never agree to things like expelling from church clergy those with Jewish ancestry, and that is what they had done in Germany. We are always only responsible to God, Barth said, and when someone claims to speak on God's behalf, a Christian must resist that person as a matter of principle. Regardless of the cost. As Barth developed this mindset, he became almost theologically allergic to presumptuous talk about God.

Still, Barth thought there is one particular thing we can predict about God, namely that whatever God chooses to do or say, it will always point to Christ. The New Testament tells us Christ is God's spoken word and we can therefore know that whenever God opens his mouth, it is Christ—the word of God—that comes out. The point of this is not to be missed. It means that when we receive the word of God, we will experience it as an actual event in our lives. It does not only result in cognitive understand-ing for us, but also gives us the experience of a real encounter with a God who acts and initiates. "The Word of God is itself the act of God,"[29] which is another way for Barth to say that we must always think of Christ and divine freedom as inseparable. When God freely chooses to act, it always involves a revelation of Christ in one way or another.

If these theological technicalities are too complex, this next point is perhaps a good short-cut description of the same. When God reveals himself to me, Christ enters my life with such force that I cannot resist it, and I find myself in a personal crisis. This, as Trevor Hart puts it, "calls forth a response either of faith and obedience or of unbelief."[30] In a way I cannot explain, when Christ comes to me, then I have no choice but to decide either that I will reject him or accept him. This is why we call Barth's theology a crisis theology. God reveals himself and that puts me in a personal crisis where I must make a choice.

It is important for Barth to emphasize that God is always the one who initiates and who gets me actively involved when he reveals himself. It is never the other way around, because I cannot plan a revelation of God and then expect that God will show up. This would only amount to a presumptuous attempt to manipulate God.

Back to the youth camp and the spiritual manipulation I could not resist. First of all, I decided to attend it because I was intrigued by the faith two of my friends had been picking up at the time. They were talking about God as if they had seen him and this made me curious enough to join them at this camp. I had seen some of the attendees before, because they lived where I grew up, but I cannot say I knew any of them.

The best way to describe my curiosity about these new Christian acquaintances is to say that I wanted their faith, but did not want to be like them. I did not doubt the authenticity of the relationship they claimed to have with God, but the things it made them do were not attractive to me. One young woman said she was head over heels in love with Jesus, and everything about her behavior seemed to confirm it. Including her disinterest in men her own age. When she and others said God had spoken to them or that they had seen him, my problem was not unbelief. My problem was the fact that they sounded naive and sometimes unintelligent.

During one of the group meetings, for instance, an impassioned young man stood up and started swaying from side to side, singing out loudly what the Lord had revealed to him the previous morning. He was wearing pajamas pants and a pair of oversize slippers with a bobbing tiger's head on each. On top of this, his account lacked coherence. I was not convinced that his words were inspired by the God of theologians like St. Augustine and St. Thomas Aquinas, whom I was reading at the time. At the same time, it was clear both his experience and his intentions were genuine.

I did not give much thought to social loneliness at the time, but knew these over-the-top Christians had something I did not have. It was not difficult to understand what they said, and they were nice, welcoming people. It was just that they looked at one another in ways they did not look at me. They shared an experience I did not have and it was clear I did not belong in their fellowship. I could not quite understand what separated us, but it caused a new kind of loneliness in me. Plus, it challenged my confidence that social belonging was something I could get if I wanted it. It had never been difficult for me to create new social connections, but with this group of Christians, I ran into a wall of exclusion, and it did not seem like something they intentionally put out against me. It was just there, and I wanted to get on the other side of it. So, I went to bed the first night of the camp and formulated my life's first prayer. I said to God, "Before I leave this place, give me what they have."

The senior leader of the camp was right on task and did what he could to ensure that everyone at the camp had the opportunity to be baptized in the Holy Spirit, if that was a new thing for them. After a few minutes' conversation with me, I had become a fix point for him and he made sure to talk to me about the importance of using the Holy Spirit as one's source of spiritual inspiration. His invasive manners annoyed me, and I gave him just enough attention to feel I could otherwise avoid him.

Toward the end of the last evening, however, he finally pulled me aside for a more serious talk. We were sitting in the main area where others were chatting and hanging out in small groups. Wasting no time, he repeated to me what Jesus told his disciples before leaving them: "Stay here in the city until you have been clothed with power from on high."[31] He explained that all Christians must wait for God to empower them before they can do worthwhile work in the Kingdom. He also explained that the "power from on high" was the Holy Spirit. Finally, he ensured me that being clothed with this power is the same as being baptized in the Holy Spirit. Then he asked permission to so baptize me by the laying on of hands.

Without much room to refuse, I decided the best way to get rid of him was to comply. So, I said yes. By his instruction we both bowed our heads, he prayed for me to be baptized in the Holy Spirit, and I quietly stared at the floor. It lasted only a few minutes, but I remember thinking and feeling nothing. Except, I did feel sorry for him that nothing seemed to be happening. I figured that was his problem, however, not mine, and he did not seem to care either way. Finally, he left me alone.

The next day was Easter Sunday and the last day of the camp. We were supposed to wrap up our time together with a large group meeting.

Those to whom God had revealed something were to come forward and share it with the whole group. The leader who had prayed with me the night before was in charge. He facilitated the meeting by walking back and forth at the front. He asked someone to share, then guided the group in a cheering applause, walked across the room, and encouraged others to come forward and share their spiritual experience too. After a while, he started to turn around and look straight at me every time he reached one side of the room. He was trying to catch my eyes and I avoided it as much as possible.

The need for people to share died out, but my man in the front still walked back and forth, explaining that we needed to hear from everyone. He repeated several times that some had still not shared their experience, and then he made a slight turn and stared directly at me. He was relentless, but I had nothing to say. It felt like we were testing each other's strengths, the way two animals anticipate a fight but still hope the other one will back down before it comes to that. Already having the upper hand because he was older and in a position of leadership, he won. Once again I figured I would give him what he wanted, so I walked up to the front and said, "I have been baptized in the Holy Spirit." Those were the magic words. He and everyone else cheered, he closed the meeting, and all of us gathered our things and prepared to return home.

I cannot speak on Barth's behalf, but I think he would voice some serious concerns about my experience. First of all, he did not consider the Holy Spirit particularly significant in our individual relationship with God. He thought we have everything we need if we have the Father and the Son. We do not also need a special anointing by the Holy Spirit.[32] Secondly, he would probably have critiqued this youth camp leader for his presumptuous personal attitude, more than his enthusiasm for the Holy Spirit. Just as he was more concerned about the Nazis' manipulation of the German Christians than what they actually said about the Jews. He would probably have said to this youth camp leader that to force certain spiritual experiences on others is an attempt to manipulate God. If I had studied Barth's theology more closely before attending the youth camp, I would have understood this better. Plus, it could have helped me establish more protective boundaries around myself.

The more I learned about Barth, however, the more I also realized that his theology had some weaknesses. I now want to look at these, because knowing about them has helped me understand something that happened to me at the youth camp and that Barth's theology does not account for.

One of Barth's strongest opponents was Emil Brunner. The two of them used each other as conversation partners but kept butting heads over this one particular question: Do we have a natural ability to know and see God, without God revealing himself to us? In theological terms, they wanted to settle whether or not we have what the German language calls an *Anknüpfungspunkt*. The best way to translate this term is to describe it as a point of contact where we can know God almost intuitively. Not having such a point of contact makes us entirely dependent upon God revealing himself to us in a special way, because otherwise we would be unable to know him. Barth said we do not have a point of contact with God. Brunner said we do.

In his essay, *Nature and Grace*, Brunner illustrated our point of contact with God by comparing us to inanimate objects. He said we humans can receive from God, but inanimate objects cannot. In his words, "No one who agrees that only human subjects but not stocks and stones can receive the Word of God and the Holy Spirit can deny that there is such a thing as a point of contact."[33] Barth disagreed, although for him it was not about a cognitive ability that humans have and stones do not. It was about God being the only one with the power to initiate a contact with human beings. The way he made this counter-point against Brunner was to publish a small book with the title, *No!*

As already indicated, I should have responded to the youth camp leader with this kind of a *No!* I should have asked him why he thought the Holy Spirit needs our assistance in order to come into our lives. I could even have quoted Barth directly and asked how any of us can know what God desires "*before* and *beside* the 'demonstration of the Spirit and of power.'"[34] This is a demonstration of the spirit that only God can initiate anyway. So, I should have said that we can baptize each other in the Holy Spirit all we want, but that until God decides to send the Spirit, our efforts only amount to immature attempts at manipulating God.

Still, something had happened to me that does not fit the picture of all these things that I should have said. It was impossible for anyone there to know, but when I had said those magic words in front of the group, and I sat back down in my chair, something changed in me. It was as if my spiritual sensitivity went from seeing the world in black and white to seeing it in color. Or, rather, it was as if what I had always believed about

God, I now knew was true. Not just true in general but true for me and I knew I had become one of those Christians I did not want to be like. The point I want to make is that the way this happened was an example of Brunner's *Anknüpfungspunkt* in action. I initially had an inkling about God, and when I started exploring the possibility that God might reveal himself to me, that is what he did. That inkling was my point of contact and when I acted on it, God was revealed to me.

From the vantage point of some years of reflection, I now think of this conversion as my first real experience with the act of repentance, and Brunner captures what I mean when he says the following. "Repentance is the opening of the heart, that is, the whole person for God, the decramping of the heart that was previously cramped."[35] As I see it, decramping is what started to happen when I stood up and spoke as if I believed. It was a limp opening of my whole person to God, but it was deliberate and it was enough to establish an opening between myself and the God I wanted to believe.

I was later to become more specific about my sins and how to repent of them, but I believe this first act of repentance is what released the Holy Spirit to live in me. Much more so than my baptism in the Holy Spirit. Brunner affirms this sentiment and talks about repentance and the indwelling of the Holy Spirit as two sides of the same coin. In his short sermon, *How Do We Receive the Holy Spirit?*, he supports his position by reference to this New Testament passage: "Repent, and be baptized . . . and you will receive the gift of the Holy Spirit."[36] For Brunner, whether or not we receive the Holy Spirit is conditional on our genuine act of repentance much more than the tricks we perform in order to generate a spiritual experience.

I believe this is the reason my conversion experience gave me a sense of social belonging that I had not known before. I felt socially excluded from the fellowship of other believers when I arrived at the youth camp, but not when I left. And I have never felt excluded since then, whether or not I would otherwise agree with details of a community's theology. It is not that Christians have become friendlier or more welcoming toward me, because they have not. They are just as all other people, sometimes friendly, and sometimes not. It is the sharing in the fellowship of the Holy Spirit that makes the difference.

Yes, the fellowship of the Holy Spirit does heal social loneliness.

Conclusion

IF YOU HAVE THE courage to face your loneliness, then you are privileged in a way many are not. I am talking about the privilege of having an experience you would never voluntarily choose, but which you do not want to be without, now that you have it.

St. Paul had a near-death experience he thought about in this way. It was such an important event for him that scholars think it divided his life into a before and an after. It happened when he and some others were traveling in Asia, and he later sent a letter to his Christian friends in Corinth to tell them about it. He wrote, "we were so utterly, unbearably crushed that we despaired of life itself. Indeed, we felt that we had received the sentence of death so that we would rely not on ourselves but on God who raises the dead."[1] It is unclear what exactly took place. It could have been an accident, serious illness, or some kind of attack. The only thing we know for certain is that it was a close call.

It requires a chronological reading of St. Paul's published letters to see how this near-death experience divided his life into a before and an after. Anthony Harvey helps us with this. He says what we should look for is St. Paul's changing views of suffering. Before his experience in Asia, he was clear that suffering is negative and that it is a matter of sticking it out. Something better will come to us if we do this, because "our present sufferings are not worth comparing with the glory that will be revealed in us."[2] Suffering hurts, he said, but by reminding ourselves of what is to come, we get the strength to endure.

After his near-death experience, St. Paul talked about suffering in very different terms. He would say things like this: "I fill up in my flesh what is still lacking in regard to Christ's afflictions."[3] It was now his argument that Christ continued to suffer after his death and resurrection because that is how he continued God's work of redeeming people. Our suffering is a contribution to these sufferings, and that means whatever we suffer in life somehow serves the redemption of the world. Christ is still

83

working to accomplish redemption, and it is a joy that our suffering has value because it contributes to this work.

With the shift in St. Paul's view of suffering, Harvey says, "for the first time in the entire philosophical and religious literature of the West, we find the experience of involuntary and innocent suffering invested with positive value and meaning *in itself.*"[4] There is no mistaking it. St. Paul went from thinking suffering is negative to thinking it is positive, and if we are to apply this to our own lives, then we must accept that there is meaning and joy in our suffering. It is not just to be endured until something better comes.

So, why not think about loneliness in this same way? If none of us wants loneliness, and if it is an instance of involuntary suffering (both of which I have argued in this book), then I say that we must. The suffering of loneliness is no different than any other form of suffering and if Christ is using it to accomplish redemption, then it is our privilege to rejoice in it. It is then also our responsibility to stop ourselves in our tracks when we start thinking God does not know what he is doing. We never wanted to be lonely, and we do not know how to get rid of it, but we do know that God is using our loneliness to accomplish his redemptive work.

THE PRIVILEGE OF THE LONELY

The most pressing question, of course, is this: How do we know God is using our loneliness to accomplish his redemptive work? How can we be sure it is not just something we imagine? Let me try to answer this with some reflections on my own process of discovering loneliness as a privilege.

Romantic loneliness first. I am now in my early forties and have lived with the unfulfilled desire for marriage for approximately twenty-five years. I think of these years as divided into roughly three seasons. At first, I was hopeful and optimistic. My friends were getting married and I shared their joy in anticipation of my own. Romantic loneliness was more of a possibility than a reality, although this sense slowly developed into a season of more serious concern for my situation. I had more serious bouts of loneliness and a growing sense of frustration because no relationship worked out. My peers were now having children, buying homes, and beginning to settle. Finally, I entered the most painful season where despair and disillusionment replaced frustration. It was slightly comforting that some of my friends now started to have marital problems and were going through divorce because that meant we could help each other think through some of the same problems. Still, I did not feel like one of them because they had tasted the fulfillment of romantic hopes, and I had not.

What puzzled me in my growing sense of despair over this situation, however, was the fact that I kept believing my desire for marriage was God's intention for me. I am not talking about faith that God would bring me a partner, but about a deep belief that he had originally designed me for one. I did what I could to entertain the hypothesis that I was unworthy or unfit for marriage. Except, somehow it did not work. Not that I did not have a laundry list of things that make me unattractive. Everyone does. But, the evidence I had that "no one wants me" was somehow betrayed by a belief that God had partnership in mind when he first created me. Strangely, the more I grew in my loneliness for a partner, the more clearly I was aware of this belief.

My experience of romantic loneliness parallels what happened in my experience of social loneliness. Coming into contact with the power of Christian fellowship for the first time gave me high hopes for my own sense of belonging. I was impressed by the difference it makes to have the Holy Spirit be an active player in the formation of social groups, and I imagined this would make my new relationships stronger than my old ones. In fact, I thought I had found what comes close to the strongest kind of community we can have. Then I went through my first experience of a church conflict and realized the fellowship of the Holy Spirit is as vulnerable to conflict as any other fellowship. That was disappointing. Fortunately, my hopes were restored when I became part of another church and experienced the power of Christian fellowship again. Later, when I had to face disappointment with that church community too, I felt more socially lonely than ever before. Perhaps also because it coincided with a time I felt burdened by life as a foreigner in America.

As devastated as I was by this disappointment, however, it puzzled me that I reacted to it in two opposing ways. On the one hand, I wanted to give up on Christian community. I told myself that communion with God is a personal matter and that we do not need to be part of a religious institution in order to experience the fellowship of the Holy Spirit. The true church is invisible, I thought, because the Holy Spirit lives in the hearts of individual believers and is not confined by the walls of church buildings.

On the other hand, the connection I had with people I was severed from by church conflicts seemed to have a life of its own and, several times, it drew me back to them. Years ago, for example, a friend and I developed a trusting relationship when both of us first experienced God's real presence in our lives. We trusted each other not just personally, but also because of the spiritual connection we had through our faith. Unfortunately, after a few years, church conflict tore our friendship apart and we had no communication for well over ten years.

Recently, this friend unexpectedly contacted me again and, as we reconnected, it struck me how neither of us could deny that the Holy Spirit, after all these years, still lived in both of us. It made me wonder if we had ever really been disconnected. It felt like God's spirit had left neither of us, and that only we had tried to live as if we had no connection. It was almost as if our relationship was rekindled and as if reconciliation imposed itself upon us. Our communication came alive again and we were able to express sincere appreciation of one another. Whether or not we will become close friends again is beside the point. I came away with a deep assurance that even though we do not appreciate God connecting all of us through the fellowship of the Holy Spirit, this is in fact what he does. Therefore, church is never an option.

I described in the introduction how romantic and social loneliness have been more challenging for me than any other kind of loneliness. I also explained how struggling with these two challenges created a third kind of loneliness in my life: spiritual loneliness. It has been difficult for me to understand why God did not answer my prayers for marriage and social belonging. Plus, the more smoothly and even miraculously God has provided other things I asked for, the more challenging it has been to accept the fact that he withheld those two things. But, I am now at the conclusion of this book and must explain why I think of this situation as a privilege.

In order to do this, I need to focus on my experience of spiritual loneliness. The more intensely I experienced both romantic and social loneliness, the more openly I questioned God's willingness to work for my wellbeing. I never questioned God's goodness, or power, or anything else Christians believe about him. Only, I was losing confidence that God intended to apply these things to my case. I felt abandoned by God and only knew one way of responding to this situation. It was to live the life of an abandoned believer, which meant that I kept sinking into the loneliness of despair and hopelessness. Whether or not I attended church hardly made a difference. Nor did any of the other things believers do, like praying, for instance, reading the scriptures, or spending time with each other. My life had lost its vigor and I was no longer committed to the life of faith. If a monitor had been hooked up to my spiritual heartbeat, it would have looked dangerously similar to a flat line.

The spiritual loneliness of this situation is the worst thing I have ever experienced. What I did not expect would happen, however, is that this situation grew more complex. It presented me with an unexpected problem. I was beginning to realize that not only was I up against spiritual loneliness, I was also up against a faith that would not die. My faith did not seem to notice that I had no interest in it anymore, and I was caught in the web of beliefs I did not want to have, but that refused to die. It bothered me that I could not shake off this stubborn thing that stuck to my heart against my will.

I was slow at becoming aware of my faith's resilience. It started to happen when I realized I was puzzled by my own belief that romantic and social loneliness were not God's original intention for me. I kept trying to convince myself I was unfit for marriage but it did not work, because I also kept believing God had originally designed me for a partner. Also, I wanted to leave the fellowship of the Holy Spirit but was drawn back into it by the power of reconciliation and the connection I had with others in that fellowship. Still, neither of these two realizations was enough to convince me that faith had a stronger claim on me than despair. It was when my spiritual loneliness was at its worst that I encountered the most powerful evidence of that, and it came in a form I was not ready to appreciate. It was joy.

One Sunday, for instance, I attended an early morning service. I was listening obliviously to the sermon and staring just as obliviously at the crucifix hanging down from the ceiling over the altar. I was more absent to the situation than I was present. Then, at one point, the priest pointed to the crucifix and said, "This is the only thing of significance that ever really happened." I am not sure why this comment caught my attention, but it did, and I was suddenly aware of a subtle physical sensation of joy in my middle. I remembered Christ loved me long before I had any capacity to know of him, or to love him back, and the power of that memory moved me.

I did not have any desire to define myself by this unwelcome joy, so I dismissed it. There is nothing more annoying than joy creeping up on you when you have decided that hope is not for you. Yet, that joy, in the midst of the worst loneliness I have ever known, was my privilege. It slowly awoke me to the reality that the God in whom I had my faith was also the author of that faith.

END OF STORY

This brings us back to the need we have to tell our loneliness story from the perspective of the end God has in mind for us. When I presented this need in the introduction, I said that in order to tell our story successfully, we should believe the following three things. That all of history is God's story, that God has a good end in mind as he is writing this story, and that the end of our personal story somehow relates to the end of all history. Now I am at the end of the book and want to add one more thing to that list.

I want to do this by first sharing an insight from Michel Foucault. He says writing a book is like venturing into unknown territory with a personal desire to explore what is there to be found. He says he writes because he is first intrigued by a subject and wants to be changed by the process of pursuing it. In his formulation:

> If I had to write a book to communicate what I have already thought, I'd never have the courage to begin it. I write precisely because I don't know what to think about a subject that attracts my interest. In so doing, the book transforms me, changes what I think.[5]

I already shared how it surprised me that writing *The Power of One* unfolded against my initial intentions. It started out as a story of lament, confusion, and a desperate need for my loneliness to go away. I knew I was lonely, and I knew I did not want to be lonely. I knew other people were lonely, too, and I was beginning to realize how unwillingly we talk about personal loneliness. I wanted us to come out of denial about this, and I wanted to find a solution to loneliness. I had no idea what such a solution would look like and had started entertaining the thought that there *is* no solution to loneliness. Even so, I decided this was an unacceptable state of affairs. So, as Foucault does when a subject intrigues him, I started writing my own book, looking for a solution to loneliness that I had been unable to find.

The writing process transformed me and changed my thinking about loneliness, primarily in two ways. First, I recognized I would not find the solution I was looking for. One result of this was my decision to make two opposing arguments about romantic, spiritual, and social loneliness. I took each of this book's three main chapters on loneliness and divided them into two subchapters that make contradictory conclusions. One concludes that Christian faith does not heal loneliness, and one concludes that it does. I wanted to do it this way as a matter of conveying how difficult it is to find a solution to loneliness.

Second, the writing process brought me face to face with an option. After several unwanted encounters with joy, like the one I described earlier, I realized I could choose to allow joy back into my life. Those encounters with joy were not particularly powerful, but as I kept dismissing them, they turned around and came back to revisit me. In the end, I had to admit that joy has a hook somewhere deeply within me and I felt trapped by it, because things were apparently going to stay that way. This struggle against joy came to a point where I knew I was trying to dismiss not only joy but faith itself. The tragic irony of this situation was that I resisted God who was trying to give me the joy I thought I lacked because I was romantically and socially lonely. I finally had to admit that the only way to deal with the root cause of this problem, and to reverse the irony of it, was to confess my resistance as a sin. Therefore, I set up an appointment with a local priest.

I had not been to confession with this priest before and did not know what to expect. It turned out to be a brief and efficient experience. The best way to describe what happened is to say that I arrived with the burden of a life I no longer wished to live, and I left with a heart restored to joy. As I was driving back home, I asked myself what on earth had taken me so long.

So, I add a fourth item to the list of things we must do in order to tell our story from the perspective of God's end for us. It is the need to repent of decisions we have made that our loneliness is proof that God's promises cannot be trusted. If we have the courage, and dare take this risk of repentance, then we regain a vision of the end God has in mind for us. We realize pursuing that vision does not mean our loneliness will go away. It means learning to find joy in the suffering we still deal with when we are romantically, spiritually, or socially lonely.

And here is my final point. When we learn to unveil the joy of our suffering, we connect with what I have called *the power of one*. We start relying on the power of God that manifests in us as a faith that is stronger than both our suffering and our will to resist God. When we experience this faith, we also know that God's power in us trumps the power of the worst thing that can happen to us. What is more, it empowers us to stand up against outside challenges in life—just as so many historical individuals have done before us when they found courage to withstand the powers of destruction that haunted their own generation.

End Notes

INTRODUCTION

1. Eph 4:5 (NIV).

2. Muggeridge, *Something Beautiful for God*, 22.

3. Hitchens, *Missionary Position*, 23.

4. John 21:22 (NIV).

5. Nouwen, *Reaching Out*, 28.

6. Rom 8:24–25 (NIV).

7. Bader-Saye, *Following Jesus in a Culture of Fear*, 155. If you want a more elabo-rate description of the advent of modernity and how it changed the way we think about history, read ibid., "Appendix: The Deep Roots of Fear" (149–59). Bader-Saye argues that pre-moderns had an easy time thinking of history as one long story of related events, whereas post-moderns tend to think of time as unrelated and random events. To us, he says, "the present feels more and more like 'just one d-mn thing after another'" (155).

8. Bonhoeffer, *Act and Being*, 159.

9. Ibid., 159.

10. Nouwen, *Reaching Out*, 14.

11. Hauerwas and Burrell, "Self-Deception and Autobiography," 200.

12. See ibid., 220.

13. We find these and many more examples in Dundes, *Interpreting Folklore*, 134–59. It is worth noticing that there are different pattern numbers. The number five, for instance, is prominent in South American and Chinese cultures, and the majority of American Indian cultures use four as a ritual number (ibid., 135). The numerical category "three" is not the only one.

14. It is for another time to discuss why the involvement of the three persons in each of God's three acts is important, if we want to avoid a modalist interpre-tation of the Trinity. Suffice it to say here that if we force a separation of the three persons, then we are only one step away from the modalist argument that God first appeared in the mode of the Father, then reappeared in the mode of the Son, and finally in the mode of the Holy Spirit. Forcing such a

separation would contradict the understanding that God is three persons in one being.

15. Weiss, "Reflections on the Present State of Loneliness Research," 14.

16. In 1987, Weiss expected that "it will be in the neurochemistry of the emotions that the full explanation of loneliness will eventually be found" (ibid., 14). His expectations match the development of loneliness research since then. Consider, for instance, John Cacioppo and William Patrick's recent landmark book publication that maps previously underappreciated connections between the physiology and the psychology of human beings. Their book is based on thirty years of social neuroscientific studies and shows that a sense of loneliness impairs not only our thinking, our will power, perseverance, and social skills, but also our physical immune system. It is fascinating to read about their discovery that "[l]oneliness predicted changes in DNA transcription that, in turn, made changes in the cell's sensitivity to circulating cortisol, dampening the ability to shut off the inflammatory response" (Cacioppo and Patrick, *Loneliness*, 106). Cacioppo and Patrick build their conclusions on an evolutionary view of human development and argue that we have always been natural social beings. Therefore, they urge the scientific world to accept that "loneliness plays an important function for humans, just as do physical pain, hunger, and thirst, and that understanding this function and its effects on social cognition holds some of the secrets to healthier, wealthier, happier lives" (ibid., xi).

CHAPTER ONE

1. Gen 1:1 (NIV).

2. Martin Luther, quoted in Bonhoeffer, *Creation and Fall*, 31.

3. Roberts, *Creation and Covenant*, 186.

4. Gen 2:18 (NRSV).

5. Gen 2:18 (NRSV).

6. Gen 1:31 (NRSV).

7. Some scholars react to our cultural tendency to interpret Adam narrowly as "male human being," because it supports a hierarchical view of the relationship between man and woman. One example is Phyllis Trible who argues that the word Adam refers to the first human being—"the man"—who was neither male nor female, but an androgynous being who then split into man and woman. She says man and woman are naturally attracted to each other because they want to return to the androgynous state of being they had in the beginning. To make this argument, she relies on the quote that man "clings to his wife, and they become one flesh" (Gen 2:24 [NRSV]). The attraction and the clinging is an expression of man and woman's desire to return to their

original androgynous state of being. Her point is that humans instinctively desire to return to the oneness they first experienced at creation. See Trible, "Eve and Adam," 430–38. Trible's interpretation deserves serious attention, especially considering the fact that Adam does not necessarily refer to one male person called Adam. According to Wilhelm Gesenius, the term *Adam* has four meanings. Adam can refer to 1) the human being as species, 2) man, as in "male human being," 3) the first human being, who is the man we call Adam, or 4) the individual human being as such, except when the word has this fourth meaning, it is often prefixed by *ben-* (Gesenius, *Hebräisches und Aramäisches Handwörterbuch*, 1:15). The first of these four meanings supports Trible's argument that the two sexes were indistinct within the first human being. As we shall see, it also reflects John Paul II's view, which I use in the next section, "True: Marriage Heals Romantic Loneliness."

8. Gen 3:16 (NRSV).

9. Gen 1:26 (NRSV).

10. Du Maurier, *Rebecca*, 236.

11. The increasing number of people who either choose the single lifestyle, or cohabitate without marrying, is easily an indication of this same tendency. Surely, an effective way to protect oneself against the pain of divorce is to stay away from marriage and other intimate relationship commitments.

12. Hulme, *Creative Loneliness*, 44.

13. Rubenstein and Shaver, *In Search of Intimacy*, 21.

14. Ibid., 22. Of course, intimacy comes and goes, as this couple admits. When they lack a sense of intimacy, they simply call it one of their "blah times," and then decide to do something that will bring them back together. Over the years, they have both developed a strong trust (even during their "blah times") that intimacy will return. They only have to work on it and wait for it to return. Sometimes, they say, it requires nothing more than spending time together, and then it comes back.

15. Miller, *Blue Like Jazz*, 142.

16. Ibid., 142.

17. Merton, *Intimate Merton*, 307.

18. Ibid., 307.

19. Ibid., 317.

20. Ibid., 285.

21. John Paul II, *Man and Woman*, 156.

22. So far, I have omitted mentioning the fact that Genesis contains two different creation accounts. In the first account, God announces the creation of more than one human being ("in *our* image"). The second account takes a

stronger trial and error approach and it is here that we find God's comment about Adam's aloneness not being a good thing. The first account emphasizes a premeditated order of creation, while the second emphasizes an organic or artistic process of creation. The two do not necessarily exclude each other, although it does pose a challenge that they are so significantly different.

23. The text puts it this way: "So God created humankind in his image, in the image of God he created them; male and female he created them" (Gen 1:27 [NRSV]). We find the first creation story in Gen 1:1—2:3, and the second in Gen 2:4–25.

24. Gen 2:19 (NRSV).

25. In John Paul II's words, we watch how Adam, the first human being, "with the first act of self-consciousness, 'distinguishes himself' before God-Yahweh . . . [and] reveals himself to himself and at the same time affirms himself in the visible world as a 'person.'" John Paul II, *Man and Woman*, 150.

26. Ibid., 159.

27. It is important to note John Paul II does not claim that the first human being was a sexless, androgynous being. Nor does he claim that it was a being of two sexes. He merely emphasizes that Adam went through a process of maturation as a human being, not as a male being.

28. Ibid., 166.

29. I group all three together, knowing that, for the single man, the actual experience of intimacy still figures in his life as a hope, not yet as the fulfillment of that hope.

CHAPTER TWO

1. Augustine, *Confessions*, 3.

2. If you want to explore this idea of despair as a deliberate attitude of resistance, I suggest reading Josef Pieper's essay, *On Hope*. Here is one formulation of his argument that captures the point well: "Today when we speak of despair we are usually referring to a psychological state into which an individual 'falls' almost against his will. As it is here used, however, the term describes a decision of the will. Not a mood, but an act of the intellect. Hence not something into which one falls, but something one posits" (Pieper, *On Hope*, 48).

3. Cassell, "Nature of Suffering," 641. This is how Cassell conceptualizes suffering, as opposed to pain: "Most generally, suffering can be defined as the state of severe distress associated with events that threaten the intactness of the person" (ibid., 640). Of course, how we understand this definition depends on the meaning of "person." Cassell gives us his interpretation when he says that people report suffering "when they feel out of control, when the pain is

overwhelming, when the source of the pain is unknown, when the meaning of the pain is dire, or when the pain is chronic" (641).

4. Following St. Thomas Aquinas, "Patience (*patientia*) has the same root as *pati* (to suffer) and *passio*, the Aristotelian category that describes receiving the results of action. Understood etymologically, patience is the virtue of 'suffering' well" (Pope, *Ethics of Aquinas*, 314).

5. Moltmann, *In the End—The Beginning*, 116.

6. Phil 1:16 (NIV).

7. One effective way of replacing this missing link is to speculate about some kind of intermediate state between death and resurrection where God will make up for the opportunity of life that some people miss. Along these lines, Moltmann imagines "that intermediate state as a wide space for living in which the life which was cut short and destroyed here can develop freely" (Moltmann, *In the End—The Beginning*, 117). He prefers thinking of this place in John Calvin's terms as a great "wakefulness of the soul," which is different from Martin Luther's idea of "life after death" as a "sleep." It is also different from the Catholic idea of purgatory, and the doctrine of reincarnation from other world religions.

8. Moltmann, *Crucified God*, 215.

9. Ibid., 222.

10. The more theologically technical part of Moltmann's argument rests on his critique of the early Church Fathers' teachings about Christ's dual nature (fully divine and fully human). The Church Fathers taught that God's incarnation in Jesus Christ was an incomprehensible, but a no less real "ontological union between the divinity and humanity" (Weinandy, *Does God Suffer?*, 177). They did not teach that Jesus was a hybrid of the divine and the human, but that he was truly, fully, really, and simultaneously both. This, as we recall, is to communicate in idioms and, as Weinandy emphasizes, it sparked the Christological controversies. Moltmann contests this teaching because it means that we can only understand God's suffering as a paradox. If we believe the Church Fathers, we have to say that God suffered on the cross, but that somehow he was still divine enough to avoid the full impact of the crucifixion. In technical terms, this is to say that God is impassible. If it is true that God is impassible, however, then he did not "really" suffer during the crucifixion, and then the crucifixion makes no sense to Moltmann. Either God died on the cross, or he did not. In short, Moltmann refuses to think of God's death as a paradox the way the Church Fathers did. It really happened, he says. God was crucified. For more details on Moltmann's critique of the early Christian doctrine of Christ's dual nature, see Bauckham, *Theology of Jürgen Moltmann*, 47–69.

11. For a theological discussion of the significance of Jesus' cry on the cross, see Rosse, *Cry of Jesus*.

12. Kolodiejchuk, *Mother Teresa*, 232.

13. Ibid., 164.

14. Ibid., 187.

15. Ibid.

16. *Mother Teresa*, DVD.

17. Kolodiejchuk, *Mother Teresa*, 250.

18. *Mother Teresa*, DVD. In line with this, Mother Teresa intentionally brought poverty upon herself so she would be forced to rely on God's provision. It is quite a scene to watch her receive the generous donation of a church building where her immediate response was getting out her tools and stripping the rooms of all unnecessary luxury. Things like pews and carpet made the place too elegant and had to go. She literally threw them out the window. Asked about this attitude of self-imposed poverty, she responds that air-conditioning and hot water are good things, but that her community has vowed to identify with the poor and therefore cannot bring such things into their lives.

19. Wiesel, *Night*, 45.

20. Kolodiejchuk, *Mother Teresa*, 331.

21. *Mother Teresa*, DVD. This documentary film was shot over a five year period.

22. *Mother Teresa: The Legacy*, DVD. "In his anguish he prayed more earnestly, and his sweat became like great drops of blood falling down on the ground" (Luke 22:44 [NRSV]).

23. Dr. Quantz made this comment in her response to my presentation, "Lonely in Faith."

24. John Paul II, *Salvifici Doloris*, 24. We find this idea in the famous passage from St. Paul where he says, "I am now completing what is lacking in Christ's afflictions for the sake of his body, that is, the Church" (Col 1:24 [NRSV]). John Paul II unfolds this further by saying that "*to suffer* means to become particularly *susceptible*, particularly *open to the working of the salvific powers of God*, offered to humanity in Christ" (John Paul II, *Salvifici Doloris*, 23).

25. Ibid., 26.

26. Ibid.

27. Col 1:24 (NRSV).

28. John Paul II, *Salvifici Doloris*, 27.

29. Kolodiejchuk, *Mother Teresa*, 259–60.

CHAPTER THREE

1. Slater, *Pursuit of Loneliness*, xxii.

2. Pappano, *Connection Gap*, 8. Italics mine.

3. Ibid., 39.

4. McPherson, Smith-Lovin and Brashears, "Social Isolation in America," 353.

5. Vedantam, "Social Isolation Growing in U.S., Study Says," A03.

6. According to the 2000 U.S. census, about 25 percent of American households now has only one occupant. This is a significant increase from 7 percent in 1940. During that time period of sixty years, the number has more than tripled, and more Americans now live alone than at any other time in history. See U.S. Census Bureau, "Historical Census of Housing Tables."

7. Putnam, *Bowling Alone*, 54–55. The exact numbers vary depending on the individual organizations. Why the drop happened is largely a mystery, except it was probably a natural development of one generation rolling into the next. Putnam roughly estimates that pressures of time and money count for 10 percent of the decrease in social group membership; that suburbanization, commuting, and sprawl count for another 10 percent; that the effect of electronic entertainment (mostly TV) counts for about 25 percent; and that natural generational change counts for 50 percent. See ibid., 283.

8. This was around the turn of the last century which, as Putnam says, was "a period uncannily like our own" (ibid., 367). At that time, America was in the midst of extraordinary technological and economic growth, received a large number of immigrants, and saw the mind-boggling new wealth of economic stars like Rockefeller and Carnegie. Urban areas and the dream of fast success attracted people like magnets, but it also caused some less attractive social changes. One of these was an increased sense of alienation and loneliness. But, even as this problem developed, so did its solution, namely the appearance of groups like Boy Scouts, Red Cross and Lions Club. People were lonely, but started organizing themselves. It was as simple as that, and who says it could not happen again?

9. Putnam and Feldstein, *Better Together,* 4. Putnam uses the term "social capital" to say that social networks have particular value for us. We become more productive and effective in our lives when we have social connections. I find it interesting that the term has been invented independently at least six times and in different contexts during the twentieth century, and each time with the same purpose, namely "to call attention to the ways in which our lives are made more productive by social ties" (Putnam, *Bowling Alone*, 19). This also means that when we are socially lonely, we become less productive, less effective, and generally more criminal. "Criminologists . . . have shown that the crime rate in a neighborhood is lowered when neighbors know one another

well, benefiting even residents who are not themselves involved in neighbor-hood activities" (Putnam and Feldstein, *Better Together*, 2).

10. Yes, electronic communication can make us lonelier because it isolates us in-dividually behind computer screens, but it can also protect us from loneliness and isolation. Before we used electronic communication to make social con-nections with other people, we had no other choice than to socialize locally. Even when we did not particularly like people in our immediate surround-ings, they were our only option for a social life. Being forced to like others is a good thing because it teaches us mutual respect and accept, but it can also be painful for those who do not fit in. They are easily ostracized and labeled "weird." With electronic communication, however, even the weirdest person is only a click away from a community of like-minded friends. See Putnam, *Bowling Alone*, 166–80.

11. Congar, *I Believe in the Holy Spirit*, 21.

12. Rashkover, "On the Loneliness of Faith," 437.

13. Congar, *I Believe in the Holy Spirit*, 21.

14. Rom 1:19 (NRSV). See Barth, "Der Christ in der Gesellschaft," 29.

15. Bonhoeffer, *Creation and Fall*, 97.

16. Ibid., 122.

17. Buber, *I and Thou*, 87.

18. Ibid., 112.

19. Clifford Green draws this contrast between Buber and Bonhoeffer when he says Buber's "aim is to create a realm of intimacy between persons, overcom-ing the objectified I-It world. But Bonhoeffer, who objects to objectifying per-sons as much as Buber does, stresses the other as boundary and barrier to the self—he emphasizes ethical encounter rather than intimacy" (Green, "Human Sociality and Christian Community," 116).

20. Barth, "Der Christ in der Gesellschaft," 29. My translation.

21. We find this idea in several places in St. Paul's letters, for instance 1 Cor 3:16, 6:19, 12:2; 2 Cor 6:16; Eph 5:30.

22. Bonhoeffer, *Sanctorum Communio*, 138.

23. Luke 17:20–21 (NRSV).

24. Bonhoeffer, *Sanctorum Communio*, 145.

25. Ibid., 118.

26. Green, *Bonhoeffer*, 49.

27. Ibid., 49.

28. Barth, *Church Dogmatics* 1/1:60.

29. Ibid., 163.

30. Hart, "Revelation," 48.

31. Luke 24:49 (NRSV).

32. To Barth, the Holy Spirit is not as much the third person of the Trinity as the *relationship* between the person of the Father and the person of the Son. "The 'inner-divine' fellowship of Father and Son in the Spirit is, Barth therefore says, merely 'two-sided,' since the Spirit is the fellowship itself" (Jenson, "Karl Barth," 34).

33. Brunner and Barth, *Natural Theology*, 31.

34. Ibid., 92. Italics mine.

35. Brunner, *I Believe in the Living God*, 117.

36. Acts 2:38 (NRSV).

CONCLUSION

1. 2 Cor 1:9 (NRSV).

2. Rom 8:18 (NIV).

3. Col 1:24 (NIV).

4. Harvey, *Renewal through Suffering*, 31. It is interesting that the first few generations of Christian thinkers did not try to formulate anything like a theology of suffering. Instead, their attitude was "clear-cut: the pains of this world are to be borne in serene anticipation of future joys" (Walsh and Walsh, *Divine Providence and Human Suffering*, 141). Somehow the early Christian thinkers emphasized one aspect of St. Paul's view of suffering, but not the other.

5. Foucault, *Remarks on Marx*, 27.

Bibliography

Augustine. *Confessions*. Translated by Henry Chadwick. New York: Oxford University Press, 2009.

Bader-Saye, Scott. *Following Jesus in a Culture of Fear*. Christian Practice of Everyday Life. Grand Rapids: Brazos, 2007.

Barth, Karl. *Church Dogmatics*. 1/1: *The Doctrine of the Word of God*. Translated by G. T. Thomson. Edinburgh: T. & T. Clark, 1936.

———. "Der Christ in der Gesellschaft." In *Anfänge der dialektischen Theologie. Theologische Bücherei* 17, part I, edited by Jürgen Moltmann. München: Chr. Kaiser, 1977.

Bauckham, Richard. *The Theology of Jürgen Moltmann*. Edinburgh: T. & T. Clark, 1995.

Bonhoeffer, Dietrich. *Act and Being*. Translated by Albrecht Schonherr and H. Martin Rumscheidt. Dietrich Bonhoeffer Works 2. Minneapolis: Fortress, 1996.

———. *Creation and Fall: A Theological Exposition of Genesis 1-3*. Translated by Douglas Stephen Bax. Dietrich Bonhoeffer Works 3. Minneapolis: Fortress, 2004.

———. *Sanctorum Communio: A Theological Study of the Sociology of the Church*. Translated by Reinhard Krauss and Nancy Lukens. Dietrich Bonhoeffer Works 1. Minneapolis: Fortress, 1998.

Brunner, Emil. *I Believe in The Living God: Sermons on the Apostles' Creed*. Translated and edited by John Holden. Philadelphia: Westminster, 1961.

Brunner, Emil, and Karl Barth. *Natural Theology: Comprising "Nature and Grace" by Professor Dr. Emil Brunner and the reply "No!" by Dr. Karl Barth*. Translated by Peter Fraenkel. 1946. Reprinted, Eugene, OR: Wipf & Stock, 2002.

Buber, Martin. *I and Thou*. Translated by Walter Kaufmann. New York: Touchstone, 2008.

Bush, Michael D., editor. *This Incomplete One: Words Occasioned by the Death of a Young Person*. Grand Rapids: Eerdmans, 2006.

Cacioppo, John T., and William Patrick. *Loneliness: Human Nature and the Need for Social Connection*. New York: Norton, 2008.

Cassell, Eric J. "The Nature of Suffering and the Goals of Medicine." *New England Journal of Medicine* 306 (1982) 639–45.

Congar, Yves. *I Believe in the Holy Spirit*. Translated by David Smith. Milestones in Catholic Theology. New York: Crossroad, 1997.

Du Maurier, Daphne. *Rebecca*. New York: Harper, 1997.

Dundes, Alan. *Interpreting Folklore*. Bloomington: Indiana University Press, 1980.

Ejsing, Anette. "Lonely in Faith: A Theological Reflection on Loneliness." Unpublished paper delivered at The American Theological Society, April 24, 2009.

Foucault, Michel. *Remarks on Marx: Conversations with Duccio Trombadori*. Translated by R. James Goldstein and James Cascaito. New York: Semiotext(e), 1991.

Gesenius, Wilhelm. "Adam." In *Hebräisches und Aramäisches Handwörterbuch über das Alte Testament*, 18 vols., 1:15. New York: Springer, 1987–.

Green, Clifford. "Human Sociality and Christian Community." In *The Cambridge Companion to Dietrich Bonhoeffer*, edited by John W. De Gruchy. Cambridge: Cambridge University Press, 1999.

Hart, Trevor. "Revelation." In *The Cambridge Companion to Karl Barth*, edited by John Webster. New York: Cambridge University Press, 2000.

Harvey, Anthony E. *Renewal through Suffering: A Study of Suffering*. Edinburgh: T. & T. Clark, 1996.

Hauerwas, Stanley, and David B. Burrell. "Self-Deception and Autobiography: Reflections on Speer's *Inside the Third Reich* (1974). In *The Hauerwas Reader*, edited by John Berkman and Michael Cartwright, 200–220. Durham, NC: Duke University Press, 2001.

Hitchens, Christopher. *The Missionary Position: Mother Teresa in Theory and Practice*. London: Verso, 1997.

Hulme, William E. *Creative Loneliness: A Christian Counselor Helps You Live with Yourself and Others*. Minneapolis: Augsburg, 1977.

Jenson, Robert W. "Karl Barth." In *The Modern Theologians: An Introduction to Christian Theology in the Twentieth Century*, edited by David F. Ford. Malden, MA: Blackwell, 1997.

John Paul II. *Man and Woman He Created Them: A Theology of the Body*. Translated by Michael Waldstein. Boston: Pauline, 2006.

———. *Salvifici Doloris*. Apostolic Letter, 1984. Online: http://www.vatican.va/holy_father/john_paul_ii/apost_letters/documents/hf_jp-ii_apl_11021984_salvifici-doloris_en.html

Kolodiejchuk, Brian, editor. *Mother Teresa: Come Be My Light: The Private Writings of the "Saint of Calcutta."* New York: Doubleday, 2007.

McPherson, Miller, Lynn Smith-Lovin, and Matthew E. Brashears. "Social Isolation in America: Changes in Core Discussion Networks over Two Decades." *American Sociological Review* 71 (2006) 353–75.

Merton, Thomas. *The Intimate Merton: His Life from His Journals*. Edited by Patrick Hart and Jonathan Montaldo. San Francisco: HarperSanFrancisco, 1999.

Miller, Donald. *Blue Like Jazz: Nonreligious Thoughts on Christian Spirituality*. Nashville: Thomas Nelson, 2003.

Moltmann, Jürgen. *The Crucified God: The Cross of Christ as the Foundation and Criticism of Christian Theology*. Minneapolis: Fortress, 1993.

———. *In the End—The Beginning: The Life of Hope*. Translated by Margaret Kohl. Minneapolis: Fortress, 2004.

Mother Teresa. DVD. Directed by Ann Petrie and Richard Attenborough. New York: Petrie Productions, 1986.

Mother Teresa: The Legacy. DVD. Directed by Ann Petrie and Jeanette Petrie. New York: Petrie Productions, 2005.

Muggeridge, Malcolm. *Something Beautiful for God: Mother Teresa of Calcutta*. Garden City, NY: Image, 1977.

Nouwen, Henri J. M. *Reaching Out: The Three Movements of the Spiritual Life*. Garden City, NY: Image, 1975.

Pappano, Laura. *The Connection Gap: Why Americans Feel So Alone*. New Brunswick, NJ: Rutgers University Press, 2001.

Bibliography

Pieper, Josef. *On Hope*. Translated by Mary Frances McCarthy. San Francisco: Ignatius, 1986.

Pope, Stephen J. *The Ethics of Aquinas*. Washington: Georgetown University Press, 2002.

Putnam, Robert D. *Bowling Alone: The Collapse and Revival of American Community*. New York: Simon & Schuster, 2000.

Putnam, Robert D., and Lewis M. Feldstein. *Better Together: Restoring the American Community*. New York: Simon & Schuster, 2004.

Rashkover, Randi. "On the Loneliness of Faith." *Crosscurrents* (2003) 436–38.

Roberts, Christopher C. *Creation and Covenant: The Significance of Sexual Difference in the Moral Theology of Marriage*. New York: T. & T. Clark, 2007.

Rosse, Gerard. *The Cry of Jesus on the Cross: A Biblical and Theological Study*. Translated by Stephen W. Arndt. Eugene, OR: Wipf & Stock, 2003.

Rubenstein, Carin, and Philip Shaver. *In Search of Intimacy: Surprising Conclusions from a Nationwide Survey on Loneliness and What to Do About It*. New York: Delacorte, 1982.

Slater, Philip. *The Pursuit of Loneliness: American Culture at the Breaking Point*. Boston: Beacon, 1990.

Trible, Phyllis. "Eve and Adam: Genesis 2–3 Reread." In *Eve and Adam: Jewish, Christian, and Muslim Readings on Genesis and Gender*, edited by Kristen E. Kvam et al., 431–43. Bloomington: Indiana University Press, 1999.

U.S. Census Bureau. "Historical Census of Housing Tables: Living Alone." http://www.census.gov/hhes/www/housing/census/historic/livalone.html

Vedantam, Shankar. "Social Isolation Growing in U.S., Study Says." *The Washington Post*, June 23, 2006, sec A.

Walsh, James, and P. G. Walsh. *Divine Providence and Human Suffering*. Wilmington, DE: Michael Glazier, 1985.

Weinandy, Thomas G. *Does God Suffer?* Notre Dame: University of Notre Dame Press, 2000.

Weiss, Robert S. "Reflections on the Present State of Loneliness Research." In *Loneliness: Theory, Research, and Applications*, edited by Mohammadreza Hojat and Rick Crandall. Newbury Park, CA: Sage, 1989.

Wiesel, Elie. *Night*. Translated by Marion Wiesel. New York: Hill & Wang, 2006.